Curriculum Bank

KEY STAGE ONE
SCOTTISH LEVELS A-B

MUSIC

D0256357

EMILY FELDBERG AND ELIZABETH ATKINSON

Published by Scholastic Ltd,
Villiers House,
Clarendon Avenue,
Leamington Spa,
Warwickshire CV32 5PR
Text © Emily Feldberg and Elizabeth Atkinson
© 1997 Scholastic Ltd
4 5 6 7 8 9 0   0 1 2 3 4 5 6

AUTHORS
EMILY FELDBERG AND ELIZABETH ATKINSON

EDITOR
IRENE GOODACRE

SERIES DESIGNER
LYNNE JOESBURY

DESIGNER
CLARE BREWER

ILLUSTRATIONS
JULIE ANDERSON

COVER ILLUSTRATION
GAY STURROCK

INFORMATION TECHNOLOGY CONSULTANT
MARTIN BLOWS

SCOTTISH 5–14 LINKS
MARGARET SCOTT AND SUSAN GOW

Designed using Aldus Pagemaker
Printed in Great Britain by Ebenezer Baylis & Son,
Worcester

British Library Cataloguing-in-Publication Data
A catalogue record for this book is available from the
British Library.

ISBN 0-590-53414-9

Contents

Acknowledgements

The publishers gratefully acknowledge permission to reproduce the following copyright material:

Ventura Publishing Ltd for an extract from *Where's Spot?* by Eric Hill © 1980, Eric Hill (1980, Ventura Publishing Ltd).

Every effort has been made to trace copyright holders and the publishers apologise for any inadvertent omissions.

Dedication

This book is dedicated to Dick Addison, who convinced so many of us that we could be musicians.

Thanks

We would like to thank all those who have given us support and encouragement in the writing of this book.

From Emily, thanks go to the staff and pupils of Walkergate Junior School, Newcastle upon Tyne and the Primary PGCE students and the teachers on the music GEST course at Newcastle University for being lively critical guinea pigs.

From Elizabeth, thanks go to the Primary BA, B.Ed. and PGCE students at Sunderland University and to her colleagues on the staff for their interest and enthusiasm.

Last but not least, thanks to Emily's mum for finding out ridiculous facts for us at crazy times of the day and night, to Elizabeth's parents for the use of their magnificent computer facilities, and to all three of them for reminding us of the need for sleep!

There is an audio cassette available to accompany this book. It contains a variety of listening selections conveniently collected and professionally-produced on one tape. Each track is directly linked to one or more activities in this book and, together, the pieces cover a range of styles, periods and cultures to support the UK national curricula requirements for music. The Key Stage One Curriculum Bank Music cassette can be ordered from:

Scholastic Educational Books,
Westfield Road,
Southam,
Warwickshire CV33 0JH.

Please quote ISBN 0 590 53788 1.

Introduction

Scholastic Curriculum Bank is a series for all primary teachers, providing an essential planning tool for devising comprehensive schemes of work as well as an easily accessible and varied bank of practical, classroom-tested activities with photocopiable resources.

Designed to help planning for and implementation of progression, differentiation and assessment, *Scholastic Curriculum Bank* offers a structured range of stimulating activities with clearly stated learning objectives that reflect the programmes of study, and detailed lesson plans that allow busy teachers to put ideas into practice with the minimum amount of preparation time. The photocopiable sheets that accompany many of the activities provide ways of integrating purposeful application of knowledge and skills, differentiation, assessment and record-keeping.

Opportunities for formative assessment are highlighted within the activities where appropriate. Ways of using information technology for different purposes and in different contexts are integrated into the activities where appropriate, and more explicit guidance is provided at the end of the book.

The series covers all the primary curriculum subjects, with separate books for Key Stages 1 and 2 or Scottish Levels A–B and C–E. It can be used as a flexible resource with any scheme, to fulfil National Curriculum and Scottish 5–14 requirements and to provide children with a variety of different learning experiences that will lead to effective acquisition of skills and knowledge.

SCHOLASTIC CURRICULUM BANK
MUSIC

The *Scholastic Curriculum Bank Music* books enable teachers to plan comprehensive and structured coverage of the primary music curriculum and help pupils to develop the required skills, knowledge and understanding through carefully planned activities. These activities do not presuppose any particular musical knowledge or experience on the part of either the teacher or the children. There is one book for Key Stage 1/Scottish levels A–B and one for Key Stage 2/Scottish levels C–E.

Bank of activities

This book provides a range of creative music activities designed for use by a non-specialist teacher working with a whole class.

Accompanying cassette

Many of the activities use recordings of music available on a cassette which can be purchased to accompany this book. The extracts are generally less than two minutes in length. This is so that the children can really listen with concentration to the extract. Any longer and their attention can wander. If you do not have the cassette, you can select your own music using the guidelines given in the 'Resources needed' section of each activity. The ◇ icon shows which activities use recorded music.

Lesson plans

Detailed lesson plans, under clear headings, are given for each activity. The structure is as follows:

Activity title box

The information contained in the box at the beginning of each activity outlines the following key aspects:

▲ *Activity title and learning objective*: For each activity, a clearly-stated learning objective is given in bold italics. These learning objectives break down aspects of the programmes of study into manageable teaching and learning chunks, and their purpose is to plan for progression. These objectives can be linked to the National Curriculum and Scottish 5–14 requirements by referring to the overview grid at the end of this chapter. (The grid shows key areas of PoS for each activity, but you will find that each activity covers numerous other aspects of the Music Curriculum.)

▲ *Class organisation/Likely duration*: Icons †† and ⊕ signpost suggested group sizes for each activity and the approximate amount of time required to complete it. Some activities are written to cover two or three sessions, and you may also choose to extend other activities into more than one session.

▲ *Difficulty*: The ♩ icon denotes the difficulty level of the activity ranging from easy, through medium, to advanced. Each chapter is arranged progressively, with the easier activities at the beginning.

Previous skills/knowledge needed

Information is given here when it is necessary for the children to have acquired specific knowledge or skills prior to carrying out the activity. This section also suggests other activities from the book that would provide suitable background experience.

Key background information

The information in this section is intended to help the teacher to understand the musical concepts and ideas covered in each activity. It generally goes beyond the level of

understanding of most children, but will help to give the teacher confidence to ask and answer questions and to guide the children in their investigations.

Vocabulary
Children and teachers often have difficulty finding suitable words to talk about the music they make or hear. This section gives the key musical vocabulary which occurs naturally in the context of an activity. Some vocabulary may appear very simple but may have a particular meaning, or be particularly applicable, in a musical context. This is usually explained in the activity.

Preparation
This section gives advice on any preparation needed for the activity. The time required should never be more than fifteen minutes. Preparation may involve listening to a short music extract, making photocopies, finding a working cassette recorder, or getting out instruments.

Resources needed
All of the materials needed to carry out the activity are listed so that the teacher, or the pupils, can gather them together before the beginning of the teaching session.

What to do
This section gives clear and supportive instructions, including suggestions for questions and discussion, as well as highlighting any problems that might arise and suggesting how to solve them.

Suggestion(s) for extension/support
Where activities lend themselves to it, ideas are given for ways of providing for easy differentiation. In all cases suggestions are provided as to how each activity can be modified for the less able or extended for the more able.

Assessment opportunities
Where appropriate, opportunities for formative assessment of the children's work, either during or after a specific activity, are highlighted.

Opportunities for IT
Where opportunities for IT present themselves, these are briefly outlined with reference to particularly suitable types of program. The chart on page 159 presents specific areas of IT covered in the activities, together with more detailed support on how to apply particular types of program. Selected lesson plans serve as models for other activities by providing more comprehensive guidance on the application of IT and these are indicated by the bold page numbers on the grid and the ◈ icon at the start of an activity.

Display ideas
Where there are relevant and innovative ideas for display, these are incorporated into activity plans and illustrated with examples.

Reference to photocopiable sheets
Where activities include photocopiable activity sheets, small reproductions of these are included in the lesson plans, together with notes on how they should be used. However, in order to avoid unnecessary repetition, sheets which are intended for use with more than one activity are not reproduced every time they are used.

MUSIC AT KEY STAGE 1

This is a book about confidence: teacher confidence and pupil confidence. In spite of the fact that in 1993 OFSTED reported that music was better taught at primary level (by specialists and non-specialists alike) than many other subjects, it is still the area that causes the greatest anxiety to many primary teachers.

This book is based on one simple principle:
You don't have to be able to sing, play an instrument or be a music expert to be a good teacher of music, any more than you have to be a poet or a novelist to be a good teacher of language.

The classroom teacher is in the best position to know the children, and to be aware of their strengths, skills and needs. This book provides information, ideas and activities which enable even inexperienced teachers to apply that knowledge to develop children's musical skill and understanding. It provides clear pointers for progression, but leaves a free choice of which activities to use and which direction to take. These decisions should always be made to suit your own interests and develop any current classroom themes.

The more experience you gain of these activities, the more confident you are likely to feel. Similarly, the more you expect of your pupils, the more they will achieve. Progression in primary music is as much about the growing confidence of the teacher as it is about the increasing skills and knowledge of the children: you may be surprised at their achievements. Progression occurs when you move forward from one activity to another (links within and between chapters are shown clearly in the 'Moving forward' section at the end of each activity) it does, however, also occur when you repeat the same activity again and again. If your class wants to do 'Greasy chips' (page 41) and 'Join the band' (page 84) every day for a fortnight, let them: it will do you all good! Similarly, if you just want to dip into a range of activities to see what they feel like, feel free: you will almost certainly be covering a wide range of National Curriculum requirements and progression will take place simply through the children's increased musical experience.

If you find that the children get on particularly well with a certain activity, the whole class can take up the 'Suggestion(s) for extension', or you might prefer to use the activity as a starting point and to follow your own ideas from there. If you are not sure how to begin, try one of the *Basic Skills* activities or an easy activity from any of the other chapters, and see how it goes. It may not always work, but remember that we all have disasters from time to time, and do not be discouraged. The only difference between experienced and inexperienced music teachers is that experience develops the ability to pick yourself up off the floor after a disaster and go straight back in for more.

Moving forward
This section gives clear links within and between chapters to assist planning for progression and continuity.

Assessment
There are no separate assessment activities in this book as every activity is seen as an assessment opportunity. This is discussed fully in the *Assessment* chapter at the end of the book (page 109). This section gives varied and practical assessment ideas as well as a range of sample recording sheets.

Photocopiable sheets
Many of the activities are supported by photocopiable sheets for the teacher or children to use. However, these are only included in an activity where they genuinely support the musical development of the children. Some sheets relate to one activity only, while others can be used with several activities. Some of the sheets are primarily for assessment and recording purposes, and these are discussed in the *Assessment* chapter.

Cross-curricular links
The grid on page 160 shows those aspects of the activities which have a cross-curricular dimension, where music might be used to support other curricular areas beyond the specific activities in the book.

Learning objective	PoS/AO	Content	Type of activity	Page
Basic skills				
To develop children's ability to start and stop playing instruments in response to a conductor.	1a; 4a. ***Using materials, techniques, skills and media** – Using instruments: Level A.*	Practising starting and stopping in response to a signal from the conductor.	Whole class, then individuals leading whole class in starting and stopping instruments.	14
To develop children's awareness and control of high and low sounds.	1a; 2a; 4a. *As above: Level A.*	Using voices to explore high and low sounds.	Whole class, then individuals leading whole class in making sounds with voices.	15
To develop children's awareness and control of long and short sounds.	1a; 2b; 4a. ***Expressing feelings, ideas, thoughts and solutions** – Creating and designing: Level A.*	Using voices to make long and short sounds in response to signals from a conductor.	Whole class, then individuals leading whole class in making sounds generated by the children.	16
To introduce children to the idea of a steady pulse.	1a; 2b; 4a. ***Using materials...** – Using instruments: Level A.*	Keeping a steady beat going against a spoken phrase.	Whole class using clapping and tapping while chanting words.	18
To develop children's understanding and confidence in using rhythm.	1a; 2a; 4a. ***Using materials...** – Using the voice: Level A.*	Copying rhythmic patterns.	Whole class copying teacher, then individuals using body percussion.	19
To develop children's awareness and control of volume.	1a; 2c; 4a. *As above: Level A.*	Getting louder and quieter using instruments.	Whole class playing instruments, led by teacher then individual.	20
To develop children's awareness and control of tempo (speed).	1a; 2d; 4a. *As above: Level A.*	Singing a song at different speeds.	Whole class singing led by teacher.	22
To develop children's awareness and control of different types of sound.	1a; 2e; 4a. ***Using materials...** – Using instruments: Level B.*	Exploring instrument sounds.	Whole class playing instruments led by teacher, then conducted by a child.	23
To develop children's skills in conducting and controlling pitch and volume.	1a; 2a; 4a. ***Using materials...** – Using the voice: Level A.*	Combining different signals for conducting, and practising responding to them with voices.	Whole class responding with voice, first to teacher then to individuals.	24
To develop children's awareness of combinations of musical sounds.	1a; 2f; 4a. ***Using materials...** – Using instruments: Level B.*	Playing different combinations of instruments and listening to and describing the effect.	Whole class, then groups playing instruments led by teacher.	25
Using voices and bodies				
To encourage the children to experiment with voice sounds.	1a; 2a, c, e; 3a; 4a, c; 6e. ***Using materials...** – Using the voice: Level A.*	Experimenting with voice sounds.	Whole class using voice, then individuals working independently within class group.	28
To develop children's confidence in retaining and copying rhythms.	1a; 4a, b; 5a, c. ***Using materials...** – Using the voice: Level A.*	Using rhythms of nursery rhyme words as basis for copying rhythmic patterns.	Two sessions: whole class, then groups of four. Singing and body percussion game.	30

MUSIC

Learning objective	PoS/AO	Content	Type of activity	Page
To develop children's rhythmic awareness.	1a; 2b; 4a, c; 5e, f; 6a, b. *As above: Level A.*	Using language of a familiar story to create rhythmic storytelling.	Two sessions: whole class, then small groups. Using rhythmic chanting and body percussion.	32
To develop children's awareness and control of pitch.	1a; 2a; 4a; 5b; 6d. *As above: Level A.*	Using voice and hand movements to explore high and low sounds.	Whole class, then groups of 4/6 using hand, then dance, movements in response to pitch.	34
To introduce the children to non-Western singing, and to develop their singing skills.	1a; 3a; 4a, e, f; 5a; 6b, e. *As above: Level A.*	Listening to a recording of an Indian song and singing along with it.	Whole class listening to and singing Indian raga.	35
To develop children's experience in playing and listening to many different rhythms at the same time.	1a; 2b; 3a; 5e; 6c. *As above: Level A.*	Combining different rhythms using words and instruments.	Whole class in small groups using voices and body to produce rhythms; listening to West African music.	38
To develop children's experience of using words and voices as tools for composition.	1a; 3a; 4a, c, e; 5b, e; 6c, e. ***Expressing feelings, ideas... –** Creating and designing: Level A.*	Combining rhythm and pitch in using voice as a tool for composition. Experimenting with speaking words in different ways and using the results to create a music composition.	Whole class, then pairs using voices to experiment with new ways of saying words. Listening to African vocal music.	41
Using instruments				
To develop children's awareness of timbre and confidence in using instruments.	2c, e, f, g; 3b; 5f; 6e. ***Using materials... –** Using instruments: Level A.*	Experimenting with instrument sounds.	Whole class playing instruments, discussing sound, listening to contemporary classical music.	44
To enable the children to discover how to use everyday objects as musical instruments.	2e; 3b; 4c; 5b; 6a. *As above: Level A.*	Making sounds with everyday objects.	Two sessions: groups of 4/5, then whole class. Experimenting, creating sound-makers, listening to contemporary classical music.	46
To develop children's confidence in using tuned percussion instruments and their awareness of melodic shape.	1a; 4a; 5e; 6a. *As above: Level B.*	Playing and copying rhythmic patterns of notes on tuned percussion instruments.	Whole class working in groups exploring sound-patterns on xylophones and other tuned percussion.	49
To enable children to apply the instrumental skills they have learned.	3a; 4b, e; 5b, d. ***Expressing feelings, ideas... –** Communicating and presenting: Level B.*	Performing a whole-class rhythmic piece on percussion instruments.	Whole class working in groups playing instruments following simple grid notation.	52
To help the children to apply the instrumental skills they have learned and to appraise their own and each others' performances.	3b; 4b, e; 5b; 6c. ***Evaluating and appreciating –** Observing, listening...: Level B.*	Playing together as whole group, using a range of different instruments.	Three sessions, using whole class and groups. Listening to contemporary music, composing own versions, performing on instruments, evaluation of own and others' performance.	55

MUSIC

Learning objective	PoS/AO	Content	Type of activity	Page
Composing				
To introduce and develop the concept of playing a sound from reading a symbol.	4c; 5d, f, h. *Expressing feelings, ideas... – Creating and designing: Level B.*	Cutting out pictures of instruments and sticking them onto a photocopied grid. Playing the piece using the instruments on the pictures.	Groups of 4/5 cutting and sticking instrument pictures onto grids, performing pieces on instruments as final product to each other and teacher.	60
To introduce the idea of sequencing musical patterns as a form of composing.	2b; 4c; 5b, e, f. *Expressing feelings, ideas... – Communicating and presenting: Level B.*	Making up simple rhythmic patterns which are put into simple sequences.	Whole class, then groups of 4/5 composing and performing rhythmic sequence.	62
To develop children's ability to create atmosphere through sound effects.	2e, f; 4c; 5g. *As above: Level B.*	Thinking about sound and feeling in different rooms of the house. Choosing instruments and playing rhythms to represent each room.	Two sessions: Whole class, then groups of 4/5. Exploring sounds and composing as group, performing piece, being an audience.	64
To introduce the concept of composing a simple theme using a few notes.	4c; 5b, d, f; 6b. *As above: Level B.*	Composing simple theme using three notes and rhythms, comparing with Batman theme.	Listening to film theme, composing in the same style using instruments and voices. Performing piece.	67
To reinforce and extend children's compositional skills.	2a–c, e–g; 4a, c. *As above: Level A.*	Using task cards as a starting point for composition.	Children working independently (individually, in pairs or in groups) following instructions from task cards.	69
To introduce and develop the concept of composing, through different stages of difficulty.	4a, c; 5d, f, h. *As above: Level B.*	Using dice to go round board 'collecting' different instruments and using them in a composition.	Game for 4 to 8 players using instruments and composing piece to perform – three levels of difficulty.	72
To develop awareness of texture when composing to create a specific effect, from a stimulus of the child's own making.	2f; 3b; 4c, e, f; 5g, h; 6b. *As above: Level B.*	Painting a picture, composing using the picture as a stimulus, comparing finished compositions with Debussy's *La Mer*.	Two sessions: group/ individual composing from stimulus of painting. Discussing Debussy's *La Mer*.	74
Listening				
To develop more detailed listening skills and the ability to hear specific instrument tunes and rhythms.	3a, b; 6a, d, e. *Using materials... – Investigating: exploring sound: Level A.*	Miming playing specific instruments as the children listen to music.	Whole class listening to jazz piece, miming instruments of 1920s jazz group.	78
To develop listening skills which recognise differences in melody, such as verse and chorus.	3a; 4e; 5a, c; 6d, e. *Using materials... – Using the voice: Level A.*	Recognising verse and chorus in song and developing this into a game.	Whole class singing 'What shall we do with the drunken sailor', and playing game by tossing a coin.	81
To help children feel the rhythm of a piece of music.	2b; 3a, b; 4f; 6d, e. *Using materials... – Using instruments: Level B.*	Joining in with a recorded song by moving, clapping and playing instruments.	Whole class moving rhythmically to jazz piece, Hoagy Carmichael song.	84

Learning objective	PoS/AO	Content	Type of activity	Page
To develop awareness of structure in music.	3b; 4e; 6c–e. *Evaluating and appreciating –* Observing, listening...: Level B.	Listening to tune of 'Where I laid on Greenland's coast' and identifying recurring tunes within music, moving round circle in response to music.	Whole class listening to folk tune as used in the *Beggar's Opera* (18th century) and running round class circle to reflect structure in music.	86
To develop children's ability to use vocabulary and express opinions about the music they are listening to.	4e, f; 6a, b, d, e. *As above: Level B.*	Choosing words to describe two contrasting pieces of music.	Whole class listening to two pieces of music, discussing and listing words to describe the music.	88
Notation				
To introduce children to the principle of pitch notation.	2a; 5a, b. *Using materials... –* Using the voice: Level A.	Reading high and low sounds from a simple graphic score.	Whole class with individuals conducting, using pitch symbol sheet.	94
To introduce children to the principle of playing from visual symbols.	5a, h; 6b. *Expressing feelings, ideas... –* Creating and designing: Level B.	Using pictures of instruments to indicate when each should play.	Whole class, teacher-led activity using instrument cards.	96
To develop awareness of the use of abstract symbols to represent instrument sounds.	5b, h; 6a. *As above: Level B.*	Using symbols to represent instrument sounds.	Whole class teacher-led activity using symbol cards.	98
To introduce and use the concept of graphic notation.	5b, h; 6e. *As above: Level B.*	Drawing abstract symbols to represent sound made by playing instruments.	Whole class, then groups of 4/5, listening to each other playing instruments drawing symbols to match sounds.	100
To introduce children to a range of ways of representing pitch, volume and duration.	2a–c; 5b. *Using materials... –* Using instruments: Level B.	Using informal notation cards with voices, bodies or instruments.	Whole class or groups of 4–6, then individuals, pairs or small groups working independently from cards.	103
To develop children's awareness of formal notation.	5b. *Expressing feelings, ideas... –* Creating and designing: Level B.	Using a familiar song to discover how notation works.	Whole class following symbols on long written sheet.	105
To introduce and develop the principle of grid notation.	2b; 5b, h. *Using materials... –* Using instruments: Level B.	Playing rhythmic patterns from symbols on a grid.	Two sessions: Whole class, then groups of 4/5. Using body sounds, then instruments, following grid notation, composing own piece.	107

Entries given in italics relate to the Scottish 5–14 Guidelines for Expressive Arts.

Basic Skills

This chapter provides the basis for all the activities in this book. It explores the elements of music identified in the National Curriculum: pitch, duration, dynamics, tempo, timbre and texture, and establishes ground rules for handling and using instruments, using voices and responding to a conductor.

These activities can be used on their own, or as warm-ups to longer music sessions, but they are intended to be used time and time again and the more often you do them, the more the children will benefit.

Use them as often as you like – as a focus at the beginning of the day, as five-minute time-fillers, or as a means of class control. These activities are not one-offs to be tried out and forgotten: they form the essential building-blocks for everything that follows.

Two ideas are emphasised throughout this chapter: one is the use of children as conductors,(the Conducting sheet on photocopiable page 114 will be very useful for most of the activities in this chapter); the other is the use of a classroom music corner. By acting as conductors, children discover that music is something they can control themselves and, if a small area of the classroom is made available to them for music-making, they will be able to practise and refine their skills as independent musicians.

Children gain much pleasure simply from playing instruments so it is important to give them opportunities to do just that. This chapter shows how you can provide opportunities in a way which develops their musical skills.

STARTING AND STOPPING

To develop children's ability to start and stop playing instruments in response to a conductor.

†† *Whole class.*

🕐 *5 minutes.*

🎵 *Easy.*

Previous skills/knowledge needed
None.

Key background information
Young children love playing instruments and getting them to start playing is rarely a problem. However, getting them to wait for a signal *before* they start is much more difficult – and once they have started, they often become so absorbed that it is very hard to make them stop. This activity is aimed at developing children's self-control when handling instruments, by teaching them to respond to stopping and starting signals while they are playing.

Vocabulary
Start, stop, signal.

Preparation
Provide enough instruments for the whole class to play. You might find it useful to look at the Conducting sheet on page 114.

Resources needed
Tuned and untuned percussion, plus any other instruments you might have to hand.

What to do
Sit the children in a circle, and give an instrument to each child. As you are handing them out, tell them they must not let the instruments make a sound. Using an exaggerated whisper may help here, or you can explain to the children that the instruments always want to talk, but that they are not allowed to talk until they are told to. Be quite firm about this: learning to keep an instrument silent is an essential skill for all music-making.

Let them have a few minutes to try out their instruments (this will make a lot of noise!) then tell them you are going to teach them the signals for *start* and *stop*.

First, show them the *stop* signal: one or both hands extended, palms downwards, with the fists closed. This is a useful signal as it clearly represents 'closing' the music. (Keeping the palms facing downwards prevents it from looking like a gesture of aggression!) Now open your hands, spreading your fingers wide: this is the *start* signal. Close your fists again, and ask the children to get ready to play as soon as you open them.

Practise starting and stopping eight or ten times in succession, varying the length of playing time. Don't be surprised if they find this difficult at first: it takes a lot of practice to play and watch at the same time.

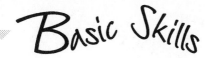
Finally, ask some of the children to take a turn at being the conductor. This can be a tremendous boost to individual children's self-esteem, as well as giving the rest of the class a refreshing opportunity to take orders from someone other than the teacher!

Suggestion(s) for extension

Children who respond well to this can practise conducting each other to start and stop when they are using the classroom music corner.

Suggestion(s) for support

The very best support for children who find this difficult is to give them a turn at being the conductor. As well as consolidating their understanding of what this activity is about, and showing how important it is to respond to signals, it is almost certain to raise their confidence.

Assessment opportunities

This activity enables you to assess children's ability to start and stop playing in response to a conductor's signal and to act as conductors themselves.

Moving forward

The skills developed in this activity are essential for almost all practical music making, and therefore come into most of the activities in the book. The activity 'Louder and softer' on page 20 takes the children forward from simple starting and stopping on to gradations of volume, while many of the activities in the chapters called *Using voices and bodies* and *Using instruments* incorporate starting and stopping signals. It is important to remember that it is not the actual signal that matters, but the practice in responding to it. Experiment with different signals with your class and see which they prefer. One very successful idea used by a lot of teachers is a STOP-GO sign like those used at roadworks. Another is a traffic light sign on which the conductor points to red for 'stop', amber for 'get ready' and green for 'go'.

HIGH AND LOW (PITCH)

To develop children's awareness and control of high and low sounds.

†† *Whole class.*

🕒 *5 minutes.*

♫ *Easy.*

Previous skills/knowledge needed

None.

Key background information

Most children know how to make high and low sounds, though they may not apply the terms 'high' and 'low' to them. This activity consolidates the knowledge they have already so that they can go on to produce and control high and low sounds with confidence in their own music-making. The activity uses voices to reinforce the concept of high and low sounds and this will help them to hear high and low sounds played on instruments and to find these sounds on instruments for themselves (see the 'Moving forward' section on page 16).

Vocabulary

High, low, pitch.

Preparation

You might find it useful to look at the Conducting sheet on page 114.

Resources needed

None.

What to do

Sit the children where they can all see you. Ask them to use their voices to make a very high sound, then a very low sound. Raise and lower your hand as they do this, to indicate high and low. The children don't have to sing the sounds: they can squeak or growl, trill or roar, as long as the sounds are at an appropriate pitch.

Repeat this a few more times, inviting the children to raise and lower their hands with you as they make high and low sounds: this helps to consolidate the concept of high and low, and gives them a physical feeling to associate with the abstract concept of pitch.

Now ask some of the children to take turns as conductor. Once the class is responding well to the signals for high and low, ask the conductors to introduce a mid-way signal for a sound somewhere in between the two extremes. This does not have to be precise: it is the *variation* in pitch that is important, not the exact pitches used.

Finish the activity by conducting, or asking a child to conduct, a repeated pattern of high and low sounds, perhaps high high low, high high low; or high low high, low high low.

Suggestion(s) for extension

Children who have shown an ability to control high and low sounds with ease can conduct each other in small groups, or can explore high and low instrument sounds in the music corner. Prompt cards can also be used to generate patterns of high and low sounds (see the 'Moving forward' section below).

Suggestion(s) for support

Some children may not feel confident about exploring the extremes of their vocal range. The more often you do this activity, the more confident they will feel. Giving them the opportunity to act as conductors will also help to build their confidence and will allow them to hear the very high and very low sounds the other children are making.

Assessment opportunities

In this activity you should be able to note whether children can control the pitch of their voices, whether they can respond to signals from a conductor and whether they can act as conductors themselves.

Moving forward

This activity leads directly into 'Pitch dance' on page 34, in which high and low voice sounds are accompanied by movements. The activity can also be repeated using instruments once children have had some experience of handling and controlling them (see 'How does it sound?' on page 23 and 'Adventures in sound' on page 44). This would lead well into 'Pass the beater' on page 49, which explores patterns of high and low notes.

The use of written symbols to represent pitch is explored in 'Music corner cards' (page 103) and 'Raindrops' (page 94). The pitch awareness developed here will also provide an excellent basis for many of the activities in the *Composing* and *Listening* chapters.

LONG AND SHORT (DURATION)

To develop children's awareness and control of long and short sounds.
†† Whole class.
🕑 10 minutes.
🎵 Easy.

Previous skills/knowledge needed

'High and low' in this chapter will give children useful experience in exploring voice sounds but it is not essential background for this activity.

Key background information

This activity focuses on the contrast between *long* and *short* sounds, which are given as part of the musical element described in the National Curriculum document as 'duration'. This element also involves *rhythms* (which are, of course, made up of long and short sounds and silences) and sets of *beats*. These two aspects are explored later in 'Copy and echo' (page 19) and 'Keeping the beat' (page 18).

Vocabulary

Long, short, signal, rhythm, beat.

Preparation

Practise the hand signals you are going to use before you do this activity.

Resources needed
None.

What to do
Tell the children they are going to practise making long and short sounds with their voices, and that you are going to teach them a signal for each type of sound.

First, teach them the signal for long sounds: put one hand in the air, with thumb and forefinger apart, and draw it sideways in a horizontal movement.

Ask the children to practise making some long sounds in response to this signal. Explain that you will stop the sound by closing your finger and thumb to 'close' the sound.

Ask the children to agree on a favourite long sound, such as a long drawn-out 'oooh' or 'aaah': you can ask for some demonstrations for them to

compare. Practise the chosen sound several times, making sure the children are watching for the closing signal and responding to it. Then teach them the signal for short sounds – perhaps a stab at the air with your fingers pointed, rather

like the movement made for throwing a dart. (Of course, you may prefer to invent signals of your own.)

Again, compare possible responses, practise the chosen sound and check that everyone is responding to the signal.

Now try alternating the signals for long and short sounds, using different combinations to create different rhythmic patterns. When the children are truly familiar with the signals (this might not be until you have carried out the activity a number of times) ask some of them to take turns as conductors.

Suggestion(s) for extension
Children who respond well to this activity can work in small groups, conducting each other to create their own rhythmic patterns of long and short sounds.

Suggestion(s) for support
Some children may find it difficult to make contrasting long and short sounds with their voices. Try giving them signals for long sounds only, then short sounds only, before giving them signals for moving on to combine the two.

Assessment opportunities
This activity offers opportunities to assess children's ability to control their voices, to create long and short sounds, to respond to a conductor and to act as conductors themselves.

Moving forward
The children will be able to use the skills developed in this activity to enhance both their composing (see the *Composing* chapter) and their ability to hear the difference in long and short sounds when they are listening to music (see the *Listening* chapter). This activity leads directly into 'Music corner cards' (page 103) in which children are encouraged to explore symbols which represent long and short sounds and rhythmic patterns.

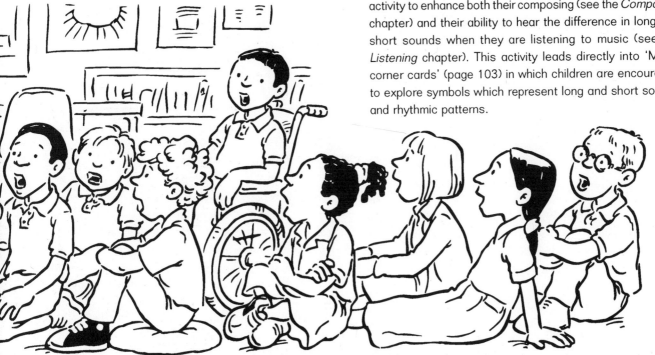

KEEPING THE BEAT (RHYTHM)

To introduce children to the idea of a steady pulse.
†† *Whole class.*
🕐 *5–10 minutes.*
♫ *Easy.*

Previous skills/knowledge needed
None.

Key background information
Young children find it hard to keep a steady beat (or pulse) without either changing speed or, if they are clapping or tapping along with a piece of music, losing the pulse in the rhythm of the music. This activity demonstrates how to keep a steady pulse going through simple spoken phrases, and helps children to hear the 'heartbeat' of a rhythm or a piece of music.

Vocabulary
Beat, pulse, rhythm, heartbeat.

Preparation
Practise this activity yourself before you try it with the children.

Resources needed
None.

What to do
Make sure you and the children can see each other's hands, knees and faces. Start a steady beat by tapping your hands on your knees and invite the children to join in with you. Once everyone is beating their knees steadily, introduce a count of 1-2-3-4, 1-2-3-4 and ask the children to count with you while they continue to keep time on their knees. If they find it hard to count and beat their knees at the same time, stop the counting and concentrate on keeping the beat steady. Ask the children to watch and listen to each other while they keep the beat going: the more times they carry out this activity, the better they will be at co-ordinating their movements as a group.

Repeat this part of the activity many times over a number of days or weeks before you move on to the next part.

Once the children are holding the beat well, try adding some spoken words in between the sets of counted beats. It helps to use words with a recognised rhythm: phrases from nursery rhymes are ideal. For example, you could use 'Humpty Dumpty':

> **Hum**pty **Dum**pty **sat** on a **wall**
> •   •   •   •
> (four beats rest, then repeat)

or 'Goosey Goosey Gander':

> **Goo**sey **Goo**sey **Gan** der **Whith**er **will** you **wan** der?
> • • • • • • •
> (four beats rest, then repeat)

Repeat your chosen phrase as many times as you like, with an 'empty' set of four beats after each phrase, so the children do not lose sight of the pulse. Ask them to join in with you, but make sure they keep the pulse going while they say the words.

Finish the activity with a final shouted phrase, or stop the words and let the pulse dwindle away to silence, keeping the same speed right up to the last beat.

COPY AND ECHO (RHYTHM)

To develop children's understanding and confidence in using rhythm.

†† *Small groups.*

⊙ *10 minutes.*

♫ *Easy.*

Previous skills/knowledge needed
None.

Key background information
The ability to remember and repeat rhythmic patterns is an essential skill in both creating and performing music, while the ability to hear rhythmic patterns forms an important part of listening. It is important, therefore, that children gain confidence in both creating and copying rhythms as early as possible.

At first, they will create very unstructured patterns, but the more often you carry out this activity with them, the more structured these patterns will become. Any patterns you create for them to copy will give them ideas for their own.

This activity works better with a small group, as this means that each child doesn't have to wait too long for a turn. However, it can also be done as a whole-class activity.

Suggestion(s) for extension
Children who have mastered the skill of speaking rhythmically and keeping a beat at the same time can add their own rhythmic phrases. Ask them to work in pairs and to hold a conversation with a steady pulse, such as

> Hello Jimmy, **how** are you to**day**?
> ● ● ● ●
> Hello **He**len, I'm **ve**ry well to**day**
> ● ● ● ●

Vocabulary
Pattern, copy, echo.

Preparation
Try out some clapping patterns yourself before starting this activity.

Resources needed
None.

Suggestion(s) for support
Some children will find it very difficult to speak the words and keep the beat at the same time. Ask these children just to keep the beat going (you can give them an important job as 'heartbeat keepers' if you like) and to listen to how the pulse fits in with the rhythm of the words spoken around them.

What to do
Sit the children in a circle and tell them that they are going to play a game of musical echoes. Clap a simple pattern, such as this one:

> ● ● ● ●

and ask the children to copy it, clapping together. Try this with several different patterns, repeating each one a few times before moving on to a new one. This helps to reinforce the idea that rhythmic patterns can be remembered and repeated.

If you have difficulty thinking of rhythms, use words from songs or short memorable phrases for the children to copy, perhaps 'Oranges and lemons':

Assessment opportunities
This activity enables you to assess children's ability to keep a steady beat.

Moving forward
This provides essential background to any activity in which the children have to play in time with each other, such as 'Percussion band' (page 52). It also teaches an essential skill for the successful performance of group compositions (see the *Composing* chapter). 'The rhythm of story' (page 32) takes the concept further by telling a whole story against a steady background pulse, while 'Multibeat' (page 38) explores the continuation of different rhythmic patterns against a steady beat. 'Join the band' (page 84) focuses on feeling the beat while listening to music.

or 'Twinkle twinkle little star':

Now invite each child to clap a pattern for *you* to copy. Ask them to repeat their pattern at least once, and question the other children as to whether you have copied it correctly each time. (It is a good idea to get it wrong sometimes on purpose, so that you can tell whether the children are listening carefully – it will also give them considerable satisfaction to correct you!) If the children are having difficulty making up a rhythm suggest that they think of the words of songs or rhymes.

Go round the circle once or twice, copying each child's pattern in turn, then finish off by repeating the beginning of the activity, with you clapping patterns for the whole group to copy.

Suggestion(s) for extension
Adjust the complexity of the patterns you use to suit the skills of the group: if the whole group is copying well, give them increasingly difficult patterns to copy. If individuals are showing particular strengths, then ask each child to copy you in turn, reserving the most challenging patterns for the most able pupils.

Suggestion(s) for support
Children often find the idea of creating their own rhythmic patterns very daunting, and this will sometimes lead them to refuse to take part. Support these children by suggesting that they think of the words of a song and say them aloud as they clap the pattern. This will help them to hear how the rhythm of the spoken words matches the rhythm of their clapping.

Assessment opportunities
This activity offers the chance to monitor children's ability to copy and create rhythms, and to act as leaders in a musical activity.

Moving forward
'Rhythm and rhyme' (page 30) and 'The rhythm of story' (page 32) explore rhythmic patterns further, while many of the activities in the *Using instruments* chapter also have a rhythmic element. 'Percussion band' (page 52) uses grid notation (such as that used to represent the rhythmic patterns here) to represent rhythms played on percussion instruments, while 'Music corner cards' (page 103) uses symbols to represent patterns of short and long sounds.

LOUDER AND SOFTER (DYNAMICS)

To develop children's awareness and control of volume.

†† *Whole class.*

🕐 *5 minutes.*

🎵 *Easy.*

Previous skills/knowledge needed
'Starting and stopping' (page 14) would provide useful experience of starting with silence and waiting for a signal, though different signals are used in this activity.

Key background information
Most children enjoy playing instruments as loudly as possible. This activity gives them permission to do just that, but introduces the essential control skills which should ensure that music lessons never turn into a riot, and that children will be able to produce quiet sounds on command.

The use of a simple signal can lead to a remarkably fine control over the volume of sound, especially once the children have carried out the activity several times. Children find conducting this activity particularly exciting and enjoy being in control. It is very gratifying to watch the conductor's smile spread wider and wider as her arms open to indicate more and more sound, and it gives small children an enormous sense of power to control so many other people making such a lot of noise.

Vocabulary
Loud, quiet, volume, signal.

Preparation
Make sure you have enough instruments for the whole class. You might find it useful to look at the Conducting sheet on page 114 before starting the activity.

Resources needed
A selection of instruments which can produce sound at a range of volumes (it is hard to make hand bells, for example, play loudly and quietly).

Basic Skills

What to do

Sit the children where they can all see you, and give an instrument to each one, telling them not to play until you give them the signal (see 'Starting and stopping' on page 14). Explain that they are going to play a loud and quiet instrument game: when you put the tips of your forefingers together, that means silence; when you move your hands slightly apart, they are to play very, very quietly and, as you move them farther apart, the sound should grow louder. Try this out once or twice.

You may find that the children are already playing at full volume when you have only moved your hands a little way. Remind them that they should only play really loudly when you have your arms stretched wide apart.

Practise a few more times, then ask children to take turns as conductor. They will almost certainly fling their arms out straight away, and will receive a very gratifying response! They may also stay at full volume for a long time, and need some encouragement to bring their hands back together.

This is fine at first, but each time you do this activity you should encourage the children who are conducting to introduce more subtlety into their signals until they eventually achieve close control over the volume of instrument-playing. You can also introduce surprises, such as sudden stops and starts, either by demonstrating them yourself or by asking the children to incorporate these into their conducting. Conclude the activity either with a final, sudden silence, or with a slow, gradual decrease in volume until the sound dwindles away to nothing.

Suggestion(s) for extension

Children who show good control of gradations of volume here can conduct each other in small groups, making very small changes in the volume of sound or creating patterns of loud and quiet or sound and silence.

Suggestion(s) for support

Some children will be so entranced by the freedom to play loudly that they will be unwilling to do anything else, and will not show the fine control needed to alter the volume of playing. The best thing for these children is plenty of practice: the more times you carry out the activity, the more ready they will become to respond to the conductor's signals. Giving them turns as conductor will also be worthwhile, as this will help them to see the need for the instrument players to respond.

Assessment opportunities

This activity provides opportunities to monitor children's ability to control the volume of instruments, to respond to signals from a conductor and to act as conductors themselves.

Moving forward

This activity provides an excellent basis for composition work (see the *Composing* chapter). A good understanding of volume control will enable children to use this in their own work. 'Adventures in sound' (page 44) also makes use of volume control, while 'Music corner cards' (page 103) explores the use of symbols to represent changes in volume.

FASTER AND SLOWER (TEMPO)

To develop children's awareness and control of tempo (speed).

†† *Whole class.*
🕐 *5 minutes.*
♬ *Easy*

Previous skills/experience needed

The children will need to be familiar with the song you use for this activity.

Key background information

Young children often find it hard to change speed without changing volume, and vice versa, especially when they are playing instruments. This activity aims to focus children's attention on tempo (speed) alone, in order to give them control over this element for their own music-making. To avoid confusion with the idea that 'faster' also means 'louder', the activity uses voices rather than instruments. It is a good idea to choose an action song for this activity, as the varying speed of their movements will help the children to understand the varying tempo of the music.

Vocabulary

Fast, slow, faster, slower, speed, tempo.

Preparation

Choose an action song which you and the children know well.

Resources needed

None – unless you wish to have the words and/or tune of your chosen song on display for the children to follow.

What to do

Introduce the activity by singing the song you have chosen in your usual way. If it is an action song, incorporate all the actions, and continue to do so throughout the activity. (Children take particular delight in performing the actions of a song like 'Heads, shoulders, knees and toes', at top speed.)

Now ask the children to sing the song v-e-r-y s-l-o-w-l-y, or to sing one verse slowly if there are several verses. Next, sing it *very fast*. Make sure the actions follow the speed of the singing at all times. Do this a couple more times, then

ask individual children to take a turn at directing the singing, telling the class how they should sing it each time.

Finish off with a full-speed romp through the song, starting with everyone standing, and telling them to sit down as soon as they have finished. (This will make the song into something of a race, and they will all finish at different times. It may sound riotous, but they will certainly remember what it feels like to sing at top speed!)

Suggestion(s) for extension

Children who can control the speed of their singing while keeping to the rhythm of the song should be able to follow the speed of the conductor exactly: if the conductor sings slowly, they sing slowly, and if the conductor speeds up, they speed up too. This will help to develop their aural perception, and their ability to watch and listen while they are performing.

Suggestion(s) for support

Some children may find it hard to sing very fast. If this is a problem, try singing the song very fast several times without the actions. If some children find it difficult to co-ordinate their singing with the very fast movements, then try building up the speed gradually, rather than making sudden contrasts.

Assessment opportunities

During this activity you can assess children's ability to control the tempo of their singing and movements, to respond to a conductor and to take on the role of conductor themselves.

Moving forward

'Rhythm and rhyme' (page 30) also uses children's songs as the basis for developing musical skills, but focuses on the *rhythm* of the words.

The awareness of *tempo* encouraged here will be of particular value for the activities in the *Listening* chapter, and any other activities in which children are required to perform together (activities of this sort can be found in every chapter).

It might be useful to discuss the need for keeping in time with each other at the end of this activity, when you have all finished singing your song at different times. This would help the children to understand the need to follow the conductor carefully (see 'Suggestion(s) for extension').

HOW DOES IT SOUND? (TIMBRE)

To develop children's awareness and control of different types of sound.

†† *Whole class.*

🕐 *5 minutes.*

🎵 *Easy*

Previous skills/knowledge needed

The activity 'Starting and stopping' (page 14) offers a useful basis for the response to signals required in this activity.

Key background information

Children love playing instruments, but are not always aware that they can play them in different ways to create different types of sound, or *timbres* (pronounced 'tambra'). This activity encourages the children to explore and control the sounds an instrument can make, and to begin to develop familiarity and confidence in handling instruments.

Vocabulary

Instrument, sound, circle, signal; also words to describe sounds such as scraping, rattling, banging, jingling, rough, smooth, and so on.

Preparation

Provide one instrument for each member of the class. Some of the information on the Conducting sheet (page 114) may be useful.

Resources needed

Tuned and untuned percussion, plus any other instruments you have to hand, including class-made instruments.

What to do

Sit the children in a circle and give an instrument to each child, telling them not to play until you give them a signal (see 'Starting and stopping', page 14). It is a good idea to give the instruments out in sections around the circle, so that all the tambourines are together, all the triangles are together, and so on. This will help children to hear their different timbres easily.

Tell the children that you are going to give a starting signal to each of them in turn. The signal will be your outstretched hand passing them as it moves around the circle. They are to start playing when your hand passes them, continuing to play as it goes all the way round the circle, until everyone has joined in.

Try this out once or twice, passing your hand all the way round the circle (you may prefer to stand in the middle of the circle for this). Stop everyone when you get back to your starting point.

Next, repeat the hand movement round the circle, but this time ask the children to *change* the sound they are playing on their instrument each time your hand passes them. They should keep playing this sound until the next time your hand goes past them.

Encourage them to be as adventurous as possible:

▲ Can they make a scraping/banging/rattling/jingling/whispering sound on their instrument?

▲ How many different ways can they hold it?

▲ How many different ways can their fingers or hands play it?

Discuss some of the different sounds and ask individual children to demonstrate.

After you have been round the circle several times, trying different sounds, signal to each child to stop as your hand passes them. (If they have already tried the activity 'Starting and stopping' on page 14, they should respond to the closed-fist signal for stopping; try using it without reminding them, and see if they can remember it without prompting.)

Finally, invite some of the children to take turns as conductors, using the same signals you used.

Suggestion(s) for extension

Children who respond well to this can investigate timbre in small groups, using the instruments in the music corner to try some sound explorations. These children could be challenged to find out how many sounds they can make with a single instrument.

Suggestion(s) for support

Some children will struggle to think of different ways to play their instruments. Try asking for demonstrations from other members of the class, and give children who are having difficulty lots of praise for trying anything new.

Assessment opportunities

This activity provides opportunities to monitor children's confidence in handling instruments, their awareness of timbre and their ability to respond to signals from a conductor or to conduct themselves.

Moving forward

The exploration of sounds is extended in 'Adventures in sound' (page 44). You can also carry out this activity with 'body percussion': clapping, slapping, stamping, rubbing hands, clicking teeth, and so on, or with everyday objects, such as boxes, books, jars, paper, chairs and tables – this leads well into 'Something for nothing' on page 46. This activity also links well with the exploration of timbre in 'Building a sound house' (page 64).

SIGNAL MIXUP (PITCH AND VOLUME)

To develop children's skills in conducting and controlling pitch and volume.

♰♰ *Whole class.*

🕐 *10 minutes.*

♫ *Medium.*

Previous skills/knowledge needed

This activity consolidates the signals used in 'High and low' (page 15) and 'Louder and softer' (page 20), so the children should have worked through both these activities before attempting this one.

Key background information

The success of a great deal of music-making depends on responses to signals from a conductor. Without one person keeping everyone together and controlling what happens, the most carefully planned piece of music can be reduced to a muddle of sounds. Young children find it particularly hard to watch a conductor and play at the same time, so opportunities for the development of this skill are provided in most of the activities in this chapter.

This activity focuses on conducting to control pitch and volume, but clearly this only represents a tiny proportion of the wide range of purposes for which conducting is used. The signals used here are only suggestions: you might like to experiment with signals of your own and invite the children to do the same.

Vocabulary

Conductor, signal, high, low, loud, quiet, gradual, sudden, pitch, volume.

Preparation

Make sure you are familiar with the signals you are going to use in this activity. You may also find it useful to look at the Conducting sheet (page 114).

Resources needed

None.

What to do

Sit the children where they can all see you. Ask if they can remember the signals that were used to conduct high and low sounds and loud and quiet sounds. Encourage some of the children to demonstrate these, with the rest of the class responding with appropriate voice sounds.

Tell the children that you are going to try to trick them by using a mixture of different signals. They must respond to the signals you give, using appropriate voice sounds.

When the activity is under way and the children are responding well, invite some of them to take turns as conductors. Encourage them to mix up the signals for pitch and volume and see whether the class responds appropriately.

At first, the children will respond to the signals in a very general way, but the more times you repeat this activity, the more precise their responses will become. It may then be possible to use more complex signals: for example, you might indicate low, quiet sounds with hands held low and fingertips slightly apart, or sounds that become quieter as they become higher. (This is quite difficult to achieve, as children have a tendency to increase the volume as they increase the pitch of their voices.) Experiment with these possibilities over a number of sessions, suiting the complexity of the signals to the children's skills.

Suggestion(s) for extension

Children who respond well to the mixed signals can be invited to experiment with combinations such as high and quiet or low and loud when it is their turn to conduct. Ask them to decide in advance the sort of sounds they want, and to work out the signals for them.

Suggestion(s) for support

Some children will find it hard to follow two types of signal within the same activity. It will help these children if the conductor repeats one type of signal several times before moving on to another. Some children may also confuse pitch and volume: it will help them to practise sounds at the same pitch which grow louder and quieter, and sounds at the same volume which grow higher and lower.

Assessment opportunities

Make a note of the children's ability to control the pitch and volume of their voices, to respond to different signals from a conductor and to act as conductors themselves.

Moving forward

This activity develops valuable skills which prepare children to respond to the signals required in the chapters on *Using voices and bodies* and *Using instruments*. It should also equip the children to conduct each other in group compositions (see the *Composing* chapter) as well as enhancing their aural perception for listening activities (see the *Listening* chapter).

LAYERS OF SOUND (TEXTURE)

To develop children's awareness of combinations of musical sounds.

†† *Whole class.*

🕐 *10 minutes.*

♫ *Medium*

Previous skills/knowledge needed

The children should have acquired confidence in handling and controlling instruments for this activity, and in responding to signals from a conductor. 'Starting and stopping' (page 14), 'Louder and softer' (page 20) and 'How does it sound?' (page 23) all develop useful skills in both these areas, and 'Signal mixup' in this chapter focuses on responding to signals. It would be helpful if children have had plenty of experience with these other activities before they embark on this one.

Key background information

This activity aims to take children's musical awareness forward, from being able to control and listen to the sounds they make themselves, to being aware of different combinations of sounds created by the whole class. It encourages them to listen to the effect of specific instruments or groups of instruments being played together, and to hear the layers of sound that these combinations create.

Vocabulary

Sounds, layers; instrument names and terms to describe effects such as smooth, busy, thin, rich, and so on.

Preparation

Look at the collection of instruments you have available and think about the ways in which they might be combined, and the effects these combinations might create. You may also like to check the Conducting sheet on page 114.

Resources needed

Instruments which the children can play easily and confidently. Provide one for each child.

What to do

Sit the children in a circle and give each one an instrument, keeping instruments of the same type together. Start off with everyone playing together, using any of the signals explored in this chapter (see 'Starting and stopping' (page 14), 'Louder and softer' (page 20) and 'Signal mixup' (page 24) for ideas).

Begin by practising starting and stopping or controlling volume to ensure the children are really concentrating on learning to control their instruments.

Next, ask one child to start playing and to continue while you signal to other individuals to join in. You can either choose instruments with similar timbres (types of sound) to play together, such as xylophones and chime bars, or you can contrast different sounds, perhaps a rippling xylophone with a banging drum.

Discuss these combinations of sounds briefly with the children, drawing their attention to whether the sounds you have combined are similar to, or different from, each other.
▲ What effect do the sounds make?
▲ Is it a busy or simple sound, thin or rich, spiky or smooth?
▲ Which combinations of sounds do you like best?

Now ask all the children with one type of instrument to play together rather than individually. (At first, each child will continue to play their instrument in their own way within the group, but once you have completed this activity a few times, you can ask each group to decide on a way in which they will all play their instruments.)

Start one group off, then add another one. Stop to discuss the effect, then start a different group and add another to it.

Repeat this several times combining more than two groups, or starting them playing at the same time rather than bringing one in after another.

Finish the activity by weaving the sounds of all the groups together, starting and stopping them at varying times so that different combinations are heard. Discuss the effects with the children.

Suggestion(s) for extension

Children who show a clear awareness of what you are trying to do in this activity can be given the job of conductor, and asked to experiment with different combinations of instruments. You could also ask these children to plan in advance, then to instruct the class, so the conductor might say 'I want all the tambourines to start together, then I want the triangles to join in. Then I want everyone to play so there is a lot of noise, then I want to finish with just one drum on its own.'

This will develop the children's ability to create and compare textures and will also lead them to an understanding of structure – the way a piece of music is put together.

Suggestion(s) for support

Many children will find it hard to describe the different combinations of sounds in this activity. The vocabulary they need to build up is not specialised musical terminology, but a range of words to describe sounds and feelings. The more times you do this activity (and others which involve using words to respond to music) the easier this will become.

Assessment opportunities

This activity offers opportunities to check children's awareness of texture and their ability to describe combinations of sounds using appropriate vocabulary.

Moving forward

Before moving on from this activity you should repeat it many times, exploring as wide a range of musical textures as possible. It also links well with activities in all other chapters, particularly 'Building a sound house' (page 64), 'Making waves' (page 74), 'Instrument actions' (page 78) and 'Talking about music' (page 88). Writing down combinations of sounds is explored in 'Graphic notation' (page 100).

Using voices & bodies

This chapter is about ways to make music using only yourself and your pupils. You do not need to be a singer to use voices, and you do not need to be a rhythm expert to use hands, feet and bodies as percussion instruments. Very little of the voice-work in this chapter involves actual singing.

Singing obviously plays a very important role in music education, but it is one of the hardest aspects of music to teach from the pages of a book. If you are a confident singer, you will probably have your own repertoire of favourite songs, and know where to turn to find new ones. If you don't feel confident about singing, first try the activity 'Morning song' (page 35), then try singing along with other recorded music of your choice.

There are numerous ways in which you can help the children to use and explore their voices as instruments. The activities in this chapter are not once-in-a-lifetime events: children will benefit from repeating them any number of times, and will revisit them each time with new levels of skill and experience.

SOUNDS IN A CIRCLE

To encourage the children to experiment with voice sounds.

†† *Whole class.*

🕐 *25 minutes.*

🎵 *Easy.*

Previous skills/knowledge needed

The children need to have some experience of following a conductor and responding to signals. The activities in the *Basic skills* chapter, especially 'Starting and stopping' (see page 14), would be useful for this. The activities 'High and low' (page 15), 'Louder and softer' (page 20) and 'How does it sound' (page 23) introduce the principles of pitch, dynamics and timbre which are explored further here.

Key background information

This activity encourages children to use their voices as instruments to create a range of different sounds. Voices are used in many different ways for music-making around the world and Western composers have been experimenting with voice sounds for hundreds of years, but there is still a prevailing view within primary music that voices should be used only for singing, and that teachers should not use voices in music lessons unless they are confident singers.

This activity is not about singing, but about making sounds. ('Morning flower song' on page 35 *is* about singing.) It explores the music elements of *pitch* (high and low), *dynamics/volume* (loud and quiet) and *timbre* (type or quality of sound).

Vocabulary

Pitch, volume, timbre and terms to describe voice sounds such as soft, ringing, rasping, and so on.

Preparation

Listen to the vocal rhythms of *Speaking with Tongues III* on the cassette which accompanies this book, or to your own choice of music (see 'Resources needed', below), and experiment with a few voice sounds of your own. If you feel self-conscious about this, practise where no-one else can hear you. Make your voice sounds as wide-ranging as possible, exploring your full range of pitch, volume and timbre.

Decide on signals for starting and stopping (perhaps an open and closed hand, or a raised and lowered hand).

Resources needed

Recording of *Speaking with Tongues III* by Sheila Chandra (on the cassette) or any other music that uses experimental voice sounds (there are usually examples in current pop music), cassette player, blank cassette (optional).

What to do

Sit the children in a circle and play them the recording of Sheila Chandra or your chosen music. Discuss the way in which the voice is used like an instrument, to create rhythmic patterns. (The piece on the cassette is based on the rhythmic drumming patterns of Indian music: the master drummer will use voice sounds like these to teach a drumming pattern to a pupil, and voice rhythms like these are also used in performances.)

Ask the children to experiment with their own voices, exploring all the different sorts of sounds they can make. Just give them one or two minutes to do this, then explain that they must each choose their favourite sound. They should start making this sound when you give them the signal, and continue making it until you give them the signal to stop.

Show the children the starting and stopping signals, then move your hand slowly around the circle, giving the starting signal to each child in turn. When you have moved right round the circle, go round again, this time giving the stopping signal to each child in turn. When everyone has stopped, discuss briefly with the class what kinds of sounds they were making, and what sounds they heard others making.

Repeat the circular hand-movement, but this time keep the starting signal, and ask the children to make a new voice sound every time your hand passes them. Try starting and stopping at different points in the circle, so that different combinations of sounds can be heard.

When you have been round the circle like this several times, invite some of the children to take turns as conductor. Discuss the kinds of sounds being made, and encourage the children to be as adventurous as possible with their voices. Depending upon the children's age and experience, and on how many times you have carried out this activity with them, you may want to introduce the terms pitch, rhythm and timbre here to describe the sounds they are making.

Now tell the children that they are going to use their voice sounds in a different way. Stand in front of the class and raise one arm in the air. Rotate it slowly like a hand on a clock-face, telling the children that they need to choose their own point in the circle, and make their chosen sound *once* every time your hand passes that point.

Continue to rotate your arm slowly a number of times without stopping, and when the children are joining in confidently with their sounds at their chosen points in the circle, increase the speed of rotation. As your speed increases, the children will have to make their sounds more frequently, and a more obvious pattern of sounds will emerge. This pattern of sounds will take on a rhythm of its own, based on the speed of your rotation. Ask the children to listen to the rhythm their sounds are making, and to listen to each other's sounds. When they can follow your arm movements confidently, some of them could take turns as conductor again, choosing when to start and stop, and how fast to rotate their arms.

Finally, listen to the Sheila Chandra piece again, and compare it with the sounds the class have been making. You may also like to record the children's 'circle sounds' so they can hear what the different combinations sound like.

Suggestion(s) for extension

Children who have demonstrated the ability to explore a wide range of sounds in this activity can work in small groups to create their own voice sound compositions. These can be performed to the rest of the class, or to another class, or might be recorded for closer listening and appraisal.

Suggestion(s) for support

Children who feel self-conscious about making voice sounds will perform more easily if they don't feel exposed. They may need extra time experimenting with the whole class before they are ready to move on to the clock-face composition in the second part of the activity.

As with most musical activities, one of the most effective ways of increasing children's self-confidence is to put them in control as conductors. This also gives them the opportunity to listen to the sorts of sounds the other children are making, without having to worry about making their own sounds at the same time.

Assessment opportunities

This activity provides opportunities to monitor the children's ability to explore and control voice sounds and to follow a conductor. You can also observe how well they listen, both to each other and to recorded music, and how perceptively they comment on what they have heard.

Display ideas

Descriptions of different types of voice sounds can be written on a large circle for display.

Moving forward

This activity leads into 'Multibeat' (page 38) and 'Greasy chips' (page 41) in this chapter and 'Music corner cards' (page 103) in the *Notation* chapter.

We made sounds in a circle

RHYTHM AND RHYME

To develop children's confidence in retaining and copying rhythms.

†† *Whole class, then groups of four.*

🕐 *40 minutes (or two 20-minute sessions: see below).*

♫ *Medium.*

Previous skills/knowledge needed

The children will need to be familiar with the four nursery rhymes used: 'Baa baa black sheep', 'Humpty Dumpty', 'Mary had a little lamb' and 'Hickory dickory dock'. Some work with rhythms would also be helpful – the activities 'Copy and echo' (page 19) and 'Patterns and rhythms' (page 62) would both provide useful background experience here, though neither is essential to this activity.

Key background information

There are two important elements in successful rhythm-making: keeping a steady beat, and being able to memorise, and repeat, rhythmic patterns. This activity incorporates both these elements. The rhythm of the words provides the patterns, and the patterns are automatically kept within a steady beat by the way in which the words are recited. Approaching rhythmic patterns in this way is easier for children (and teachers!) than trying to create them out of thin air. It also gives children a repertoire of rhythms on which they can draw for their own composition work.

This activity can easily be spread over two sessions, the first session incorporating the whole-class work and a second session for the group work and final performance.

Vocabulary

Rhythm, words.

Preparation

Practise singing or reciting the four nursery rhymes 'Baa baa black sheep', 'Humpty Dumpty', 'Mary had a little lamb' and 'Hickory dickory dock', emphasising the rhythm very strongly. Then try reciting each rhyme in your head, tapping or clapping the pattern of the words as you do so. Finally, try substituting body sounds for the words.

Resources needed

Cassette recorder and blank cassette (optional).

What to do

Session One

Ask the children to sit in a circle and, without any introduction, start to sing or recite 'Baa baa black sheep', clapping the rhythm of the words as you do so. Invite the children to join in with this, then ask them if they can clap the rhythm *without singing the words*. Repeat this once or twice, then split the circle into four. Ask the children in each quarter to copy the rhythm of one line after you have clapped it: so the first quarter copies the first line, the second quarter copies the second line, and so on.

When you have been right round the circle twice, carry on for a third time, but substitute body sounds for clapping. You could tap your head or shoulders, slap your knees, stamp your feet, or do a combination of these things. Ask the children to copy exactly what you do each time, still working with one quarter of the circle for each line of the rhyme. Go round the circle another two or three times like this, changing the body sounds you use each time.

Repeat the process now with 'Humpty Dumpty', starting with simple clapping then again exploring body sounds around the circle. Do the same with 'Mary had a little lamb' and 'Hickory dickory dock'.

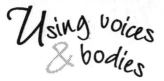
Session Two

Split the class into groups of four and assign a nursery rhyme to each group: either use all four rhymes, or just choose one or two. Ask the children to play the copying game in their groups, with the group members each taking a line of their rhyme and making it into a rhythm for the rest of the group to copy (children can double up or repeat lines if groups are uneven in size). Ask them to experiment with as many different body sounds as possible while they are working, and to choose their favourite combinations for a performance to the rest of the class at the end of the session.

Give the groups about 10 minutes to work on their rhymes, then bring them back together to listen to each other's performances.

Some of the children may find it hard to remember exactly what they did once they have heard another group performing, or they may deliberately incorporate someone else's ideas into their own performance. There is no need to criticise these alterations: the act of performing has a value of its own, quite separate from the exploratory group work, and imitating other people's ideas is a well-established way of developing musical expertise!

As a conclusion to the activity try recording the groups' performances, or performing them to another class. You can also try putting all the groups' rhythms together to make a complex rhythmic pattern, or ask them to recite all four nursery rhymes at the same time: they fit together very well, and make a fascinating combination of sounds.

Suggestion(s) for extension

To make this more challenging, particularly if you repeat the activity several times through a term or a year, try incorporating silent gestures such as head-nods or arm-movements into the rhythm. Children who have worked confidently on the nursery rhymes in this activity could choose other songs or rhymes to use as a basis for their own rhythmic copying games (the words of most pop songs work well). The children can then experiment with increasingly complex ways of combining body sounds to create the rhythms.

Suggestion(s) for support

Some children may find it hard to retain the rhythm of the nursery rhyme words. If they are having difficulty reproducing the rhythm, encourage them to say the words as they clap. It will also be easier for these children if they only have to produce one type of sound so they can concentrate on the rhythm. Let them use *just* clapping, stamping or slapping rather than a combination of sounds.

Assessment opportunities

During the activity try to monitor the children's ability to memorise, copy and create rhythms, keep a steady beat, respond to a conductor and act as conductors themselves.

Opportunities for IT

Groups of children could use a cassette recorder to record their own rhymes. They will need to know how to operate the cassette recorder, using the record, pause, play and rewind buttons. Working with a cassette recorder in this way introduces children to some basic ideas about control of technology.

Display ideas

The words of the nursery rhymes might be displayed alongside children's descriptions of the body sounds they used to represent them.

Moving forward

This activity links well with 'The rhythm of story' (page 32). Rhythmic patterns are explored further in 'Multibeat' (page 38), and the rhythmic use of words is extended further in 'Greasy chips' (page 41). 'Percussion band' (page 52) develops children's ability to keep a steady beat, while the use of body sounds is also explored in activities in the *Composing* chapter.

THE RHYTHM OF STORY

To develop children's rhythmic awareness.

†† *Whole class.*

🕐 *Two 20-minute sessions*

♫ *Session 1: easy.*
  Session 2: medium.

Previous skills/knowledge needed

The children need to have some experience of using rhythms and keeping a steady beat. 'Copy and echo' (page 19), 'Keeping the beat' (page 18) and 'Rhythm and rhyme' (page 30) would all be useful for this.

Key background information

The advantages of using patterned-language texts with strong rhythm and/or rhyme to enhance reading development in the early years has long been recognised. In this activity, the pattern of a familiar text is used to enhance *rhythmic* development, but it is likely to have the additional effect of increasing children's self-confidence in using stories, and therefore in reading.

The text chosen here is *Where's Spot?* by Eric Hill, but any strongly-patterned, rhythmic text would do just as well. This activity has a heavy emphasis on musical development rather than the more familiar technique of illustrating a story with sound-effects, but the two might be fruitfully combined to create a rhythmic and sound-effect extravaganza.

Vocabulary

Rhythm, beats

Preparation

Familiarise yourself with your chosen story. Try out a few different ways of reciting it with a strong rhythmic emphasis, but keep an open mind.

Resources needed

Where's Spot? by Eric Hill (Ventura Publishing), copies of the 'My performance' evaluation sheet (page 153) if you plan to use it.

What to do

Session One

Read the story to the class, encouraging them to join in all the way through. Then tell the children that you are all going to read or perform the story together in a special way. Start a steady beat of 1-2-3-4 with everyone keeping time by beating their hands on their knees. Ask for suggestions as to how the title of the story might fit into this pattern of beats. The children will probably come up with something like:

```
1 - 2 - 3 - 4      1 - 2 - 3 - 4
Wh - e - r - e's    S P O T?
```

Try out several possibilities, to see what they sound like. Go on to the first line of the story, and work out a way of fitting this into the pattern too. Always keep the natural rhythm of the words in mind while you are making or considering suggestions.

After you have tried out the title and the first page against the background of steady beats to see how they sound, continue through the story, working out how to 'perform' each page. The same pattern can often be repeated for many pages, as the pattern of the language stays the same. Work out with the children how to account for special features – such as the hippo and bird together in the piano, and the three penguins in the box. Consider allowing four or eight empty beats (with no words) between pages, to give yourself time to turn over. It is also a good idea to repeat each page, so the children don't feel rushed.

Towards the end of the story the language pattern changes: 'There's Spot! He's under the rug.' This signals that the story is taking a new turn, and you may want to change your rhythmic pattern accordingly. You will also need to decide how to represent the page on which Sally actually finds Spot, on which there is no writing at all. Children will take great pleasure in using rhythmic woofing and slurping noises to accompany the final page, where Spot eats up his dinner, and you may wish to extend this into a grand rhythmic finale.

Once you have worked out the whole story, perform it all the way through. You may need to do this several times to get it just right. When you are satisfied with your performance, another teacher or class could be invited to listen.

Session Two

Start this session by repeating the performance of the story prepared in Session One. When the children feel confident with this, split them into three groups: the first group simply repeats the title again and again throughout the recital, the second group recites all the questions ('Is he behind the door?' and so on) and the third group puts in the word 'No' each time, with groups two and three joining together for the beginning and end of the story. Develop this further by

adding rhythmic interludes of 'doggy' sounds between the pages or try splitting the class into smaller groups, giving some groups different rhythmic phrases to repeat while others recite the story.

Encourage one or two small groups of children to provide a rhythmic backing with percussion instruments. Again, when you are all satisfied with your recital, you can perform it to an audience.

It would be a good idea to perform both the version you created in Session One and the new version from this session for the audience to compare, or you could record both on cassette for the children to compare and evaluate. (You might like to use the 'My performance' evaluation sheet (page 153) as a follow-up to this activity.)

Suggestion(s) for extension

Children who have coped well with this activity can choose other favourite texts and work out ways of performing them rhythmically, either individually or in groups.

Suggestion(s) for support

Children who have difficulty with this will find it easier if they are paired with someone who can hold the rhythmic pattern confidently and recite the words strongly.

Assessment opportunities

This activity provides opportunities to note whether the children can keep a steady beat, recite words rhythmically and plan a performance.

Opportunities for IT

The children could use a keyboard to set up a simple rhythm accompaniment to go with the story. Older or more able children may be able to programme and record several rhythms into the keyboard memory or on to a tape to allow for changes of rhythm in the story.

An alternative approach would be to use a simple computer program such as *Music Box* or *Compose World*, both of which enable children to set up their own rhythm patterns and sequence them to accompany the story.

Reference to photocopiable sheet

Photocopiable page 153 is an evaluation sheet for children to appraise their own performance.

Moving forward

The rhythmic use of words in this activity provides a good preparation for 'Greasy chips' (page 41), as well as for further explorations of rhythm in 'Multibeat' (page 38) and 'Percussion band' (page 52).

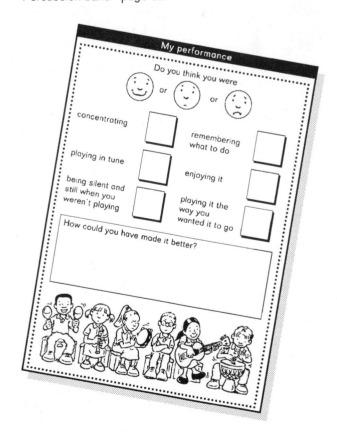

PITCH DANCE

To develop children's awareness and control of pitch.

✝✝ *Whole class initially, then groups of four to six.*

🕑 *15 minutes.*

🎵 *Medium.*

Previous skills/knowledge needed
The children need to have some understanding of high and low sounds – the activity 'High and low' (page 15) would be a useful preparation for this.

Key background information
The value of using hand or body movements to represent pitch differences has long been recognised in music education. It provides the basis of Zoltan Kodaly's influential work with children in which hand movements are used to introduce the system known as tonic sol-fa (familiar to most of us through the song 'Doh-re-mi' from *The Sound of Music*). This is also the principle behind the pitch games in Richard Addison's *Bright Ideas: Music* (also published by Scholastic).

The use of physical gestures in this way helps children to understand the concept of 'high' and 'low' in music, which is much less easy to grasp than high and low in other contexts.

Vocabulary
High, low, pitch.

Preparation
None.

Resources needed
None.

What to do
Start with the whole class together. Ask everyone to make some very high sounds with their voices, then some very low ones, then some sounds in between. Stress that they don't have to use singing voices for this: squeaks, growls and other sounds are equally acceptable. Accompany each

set of sounds with a hand gesture: raise your hand above your head for high notes, lower it almost to the floor for low notes, and place it at chest level for notes in between. Ask the children to do the same as they make the sounds with their voices.

When the children are comfortable with the combination of sounds and gestures, split them into groups of four to six and ask each group to form a star, as in country dancing (the children stand in a small circle, and each child puts one hand into the middle to make the centre of the star).

Ask the groups to experiment with high and low sounds and movements. At first, they will probably find it easier to make high and low sounds as a group, so that their hands move up and down together at the centre of the star.

At this point you can either stop the class and ask the groups to demonstrate this to each other, or move straight on to asking each child to make independent sounds and movements within their own group, so that the centre of the star becomes a shifting one, and the children's hands create a dance in the air accompanied by their voice sounds. (This will have one effect if the children keep in time with each other, and another if the children change pitch at their own

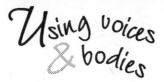

speed: both are equally acceptable.) If they are stretching very high and very low, their whole bodies will become part of the dance, too.

You can conclude this activity in one of two ways: either ask each group to demonstrate their pitch dance to the rest of the class, remembering the specific movements they were making when they were working in their groups, or bring all the children together into a single circle and create a whole-class pitch dance together, with the children improvising their sounds and movements individually in response to the rest of the group.

Suggestion(s) for extension
Children who have clearly grasped the relationship between high and low sounds and the corresponding gestures can create a more structured pitch dance: a planned sequence of sounds and movements involving repeated patterns, silences and a combination of whole-group and individual sounds and movements.

Groups could also experiment with different types of high and low sounds: they might contrast continuous humming with short, sharp sounds, make high and low animal sounds, or they might use words to create a pitch song to accompany their movements.

Suggestion(s) for support
Some children may find it difficult to make sounds and hand gestures at the same time, while others may not be able to represent high and low sounds with appropriate gestures. These children will be helped by playing copying games – copying each other's sounds and movements. You can also help them by guiding their hands as they make their own sounds.

Assessment opportunities
During the activity check the children's awareness and control of pitch as well as their ability to relate sounds to movements.

Opportunities for IT
Children could use a computer to draw out a graphic score (see 'Graphic notation' on page 100) which can be read and performed as a sequence of high and low sounds.

The children could use a video camera to make a film of their pitch dance.

Display ideas
Photographs of the children performing their pitch dances give a visual demonstration of high and low and help to consolidate the concept of high and low pitch. Charts or diagrams which could also be used for data analysis in maths could show objects or creatures which make high and low sounds. The investigation of how high and low sounds are produced could lead to a display linking music and science.

Moving forward
The awareness of pitch developed here will prepare children to use their voices in 'Greasy chips' (page 41) and to work on notation in 'Raindrops' (page 94).

◖♩◗ MORNING SONG

To introduce the children to non-Western singing, and to develop their singing skills.

†† *Whole class.*

⏲ *20 minutes.*

♫ *Medium.*

Previous skills/knowledge needed
The children will need some experience of singing, though this need not be highly specialised. 'High and low' (page 15) and 'Sounds in a circle' (page 28) explore voice control, while 'Heads and tails' (page 81) explores structure through singing. Any of these would be a useful preparation for this activity.

Key background information
This activity uses a sung 'raga' from the classical music of India as a way of introducing children to non-Western vocal style. (A raga is a sequence of notes used as a basis for a piece of music, rather like a scale in Western music.) The singer improvises around the notes which form the raga, accompanied by three instruments: a drum called a *tabla*, a stringed instrument called a *tampura* which plays a continuous sequence of notes throughout the piece, and another stringed instrument called a *sarangi*, which sounds similar to a violin. The example on the cassette which

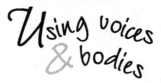

accompanies this book is a morning raga: the sequence of notes conveys the mood of this part of the day. However the activity could be carried out with any piece of vocal music from a non-Western country. Choose a short extract that uses a repeated melody, so that the children can try to sing along with it. If the chosen piece also makes unfamiliar use of the voice, such as the shimmering rise and fall which occurs in the example on the cassette, the children can also try to imitate this.

Vocabulary

Indian, raga, shimmer.

Preparation

Listen to the recording of 'Raga Bilaskhani Todi', extract 2 on the cassette (or to your own choice of music) a few times, and try singing along with it yourself. Try to imitate the shimmering effect of the voice in the middle of the extract, as well as singing along with the repeated melody at the beginning and end.

Resources needed

Recording of 'Raga Bilaskhani Todi' on the cassette which accompanies this book, cassette player, photocopiable pages 140 and 134 (optional).

What to do

Play the recording of the raga three times to the class without discussion. The first time, the children may laugh because the music sounds unusual to them (though children of Indian origin will find the music refreshingly familiar). By the third time, the children will probably recognise the sequence of sung notes each time they hear it, and may show that they are anticipating the shimmering rise and fall of the voice in the middle of the extract.

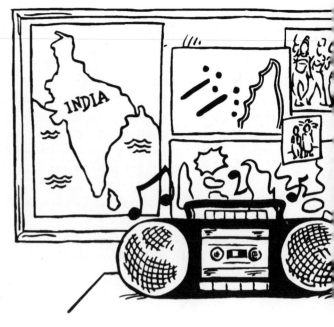

Tell the children that this music comes from India, and that this is a morning song. Split the class in half and invite one half to hum or sing along with the melody while the other half make their voices shimmer with the middle section as you play the recording again. They may find it difficult to match their voices with the recording at first, but this will get easier each time they try. After they have done this two or three times, swap the two halves of the class over. Ask the children to pay particular attention to the type of voice they use: if they don't feel confident enough to try singing the words ('Sa-ja-na-moori aaah, aah, aah' would be a good start), ask them to sing 'aah' or 'ooh' to the melody.

Now challenge the class to sing the raga *without* the recording. Bring each half in or, better still, choose a child conductor to take control. Do this several times, so that each half of the class has a number of chances to sing each part of the raga. Now listen to the recording again and compare your version with the original. Ask the children how well they think they kept to the notes of the raga. How successful were they in making their voices sound like the singer's voice? Perhaps they can suggest ways in which they might improve their version to make it sound more authentic. If any children mention the instruments at this point, explain what instruments are used (see 'Key background information') and ask the children to suggest what Western instruments would make a similar sound. (A drum, a guitar and a violin would be appropriate suggestions.) Conclude the lesson by playing the recording a final time, asking the children to listen carefully to the voice and instruments rather than singing along.

As a follow-up, the children might represent the song in their own way, using the Graphic notation sheet on page 140. Their representation might show, for example, how the melody goes up and down, or how the voice changes from singing words to shimmering up and down the scale.

own graphic scores of the raga, these could also be displayed. The display could be linked with work in RE on Hindu mythology; it was with music, for example, that the god Krishna charmed his love, Radha, and music plays an important part in Hindu festivals. Hindu art also contains numerous representations of instruments: both gods and humans are often portrayed carrying instruments.

Reference to photocopiable sheets
The children can use photocopiable page 140 to write their own graphic score of the song. Page 134 contains descriptive vocabulary which children might use when talking about the characteristics of the music.

Moving forward
The awareness of vocal style developed in this activity offers good preparation for the use of voices in 'Greasy chips' (page 41). The children's awareness of non-Western music could be developed further with activities in the *Listening* chapter, especially 'Talking about music' (page 88).

Suggestion(s) for extension
Children who have found it easy to imitate the sound and style of Indian singing could try creating their own raga, using a repeated sequence of notes of their own choice. They could use either their own voices or instruments for this, or a combination of the two.

Suggestion(s) for support
Some children will find it hard to match their voices to the notes of the raga. Place them next to someone who is more confident, to give them support. It may also help to put children who are having difficulty singing the raga in charge of conducting it: this will both raise their self-esteem and enable them to hear the other children singing without worrying about the sounds they are making themselves.

Assessment opportunities
This activity provides opportunities for you to monitor the children's awareness of different singing styles, their ability to sing along with a recorded song and to remember and repeat a vocal pattern.

Opportunities for IT
The children could use an art or drawing package to make their own graphic score of the raga. They could also research Indian classical music on CD-Rom – some packages play recorded examples of music as well as offering written and pictorial information.

Display ideas
This activity could be linked to a geography project by displaying a description and a recording of the raga along with the pictures of Indian people and scenery. (The vocabulary sheet 134 would make a useful starting-point when describing the music.) If the children have drawn their

Music words

smooth quiet busy booming rrrepeatinggggs tuneful boring spiky LOUD happy jumpy slide bold harsh calm

◆ MULTIBEAT

To develop children's experience in playing and listening to many different rhythms at the same time.

†† *Whole class.*
🕐 *20 minutes.*
♫ *Advanced.*

Previous skills and knowledge needed
'Keeping the beat' (page 18), 'Something for nothing' (page 46) and 'Rhythm and rhyme' (page 30) would all be useful preparation for this activity.

Key background information
Many forms of music use more complicated rhythms than the 1-2-3-4 that we can often pick out in Western classical music. Rhythms that span over five, seven or nine beats are common in many African, Asian or Latin-American rhythms. Often, more than one rhythm is played or sung at the same time and this creates what are known as **cross rhythms** (many rhythms of different length played at one time that cross over each other). The best way to experience the feel of these complicated rhythms is to play them.

Vocabulary
Pulse, steady, rhythm, beat, cross rhythms.

Preparation
Listen to *Salikaro* by Sékou Camara Cobra, a composition based on West African rhythms, (extract 3 on the cassette) or any other piece of music that has more than one set of rhythms going at the same time. Pop music can be a good source. Familiarise yourself with the different rhythms and read through the activity sheet.

For the second session you will need to gather enough instruments to have one for each child.

Resources needed
A recording of *Salikaro* by Sékou Camara Cobra or similar music, cassette player, an instrument (of any type) for each child, enough copies of photocopiable pages 115 and 116 to have one for each group of four.

What to do
Session One
Tell the children that you are going to work on keeping a steady pulse going. Ask them to listen first to what you do. Using two fingers on the palm of your hand, tap a steady pulse. Ask the class to do the same thing.

To encourage the idea that the children should start at the same time, count '1-2-3-4' using the same pulse for the count as for your tapping. Children often find it hard to grasp the concept of starting together, so use any added prompts such as raising your voice slightly on '4' or indicating with

your head and tapping finger when they should come in. Keep the tapping going for at least a minute, taking care to keep the speed constant – children and adults always tend to increase the pace of the tapping.

After one minute of tapping, stop the class (use a stopping sign that the whole class knows and understands) and discuss the need for a steady pulse that does not get faster or slower.

If the children have responded well so far, divide the class in half. Tell them that one half is going to watch and count while the other half plays. Ask the counting half to count 1-2-3-4, 1-2-3-4, 1-2-3-4, in time with every tap. Let each half take turns at being the counters and tappers but make the changeover part of the steady pulse. If the children find this hard, return to the whole class counting and tapping at the same time.

When the class are confident with this, encourage them to count in their heads, only saying or shouting the '1' out loud. The aim here is to get the class to say '1' confidently at the beginning of every set of four. When the children have grasped this, tell them that you are going to change the count, so that they only have to count up to three. Repeat the same process as above, tapping first, then counting 1-2-3, 1-2-3, 1-2-3, finally shouting only the '1'.

Once the children are confident with this introduce the idea of replacing the count of 1-2-3-4 with the four-syllable word,

| cat - er - pil - lar |
| 1   2   3   4 |

Say the word several times, keeping to the steady pulse you had before. Then introduce, as a replacement word for the three-beat rhythm,

| but - ter - fly |
| 1   2   3 |

Show the children photocopiable page 115 with the pictures of the butterflies and caterpillars drawn in on a grid notation. This visual representation shows that for every four butterflies there will be three caterpillars. Point out that this is how the music is meant to work and that while one group is still saying 'caterpillar' the other group will have finished saying 'butterfly'.

If another adult is available to help, ask her to point to line one (butterfly, butterfly, butterfly, butterfly) while you, on another copy of the sheet, point to line two (caterpillar, caterpillar, caterpillar). Reading from a visual representation often helps the children to manage working with two (or three) different rhythms.

Next, divide the class in two. One half will say 'cat-er-pil-lar' and the other half will say 'but-ter-fly'. Explain to the children that both halves are going to start together saying the different rhythms at the same time. By saying, rather than beating them, the children will be able to maintain the two different rhythms when they say them at the same time. It is important to keep the original pulse going – try a quiet clap or tap on the carpet. Count the children in using something which has neither a three- or four-beat rhythm – 'ig-u-an-o-don' works well as it has five beats!

As the children get used to the two rhythms ask them to say only the first syllable of their word ('cat' or 'but') out loud while they whisper the rest of their rhythm or just mouth it silently. Occasionally the two groups' words will coincide but mostly they will come in different places. The effect of this is quite amazing as there will be quiet gaps in between what seems like random calling out. This is the beginning of working with polyrhythms.

To end the session play the children *Salikaro* by Sékou Camara Cobra. This has many different rhythms going on at the same time. Ask the children if they can keep the beat of any of the rhythms they can hear and how many different rhythms they can hear. Don't be confused by different instruments and different rhythms, many instruments can

be playing the same rhythms and three drums could each be playing a different rhythm. The children will need a lot of practice in playing the rhythms before they are completely confident.

Session Two

Start the session by repeating, briefly, the work done in Session One. When the children are confident with the cat-er-pil-lar and but-ter-fly ask them to clap on the first syllable, saying the rest of the rhythm in a whisper.

Give out instruments to a few children, making sure that both rhythms are represented. Ask the instrumentalists to bang only, shake or blow on the first word of their rhythm. This means that instruments will only be playing on the 'cat' and 'but'. As the class becomes accustomed to the instruments, stop the activity and give every child an instrument. Emphasise to them that you only want them to play on the first syllable.

Practise with both halves of the class separately. Keep the steady pulse going, tapping quietly on a drum or tambourine works well.

When you feel both halves are confident, let the children play rhythms together, still playing only on the first syllable of each word. Ask the children just to say the words in their heads now so that only the instruments can be heard. This is an instrumental performance of cross rhythms.

Suggestion(s) for extension

If some children are very confident, encourage a small group or an individual to play each rhythm alone, then ask them to play the two rhythms at the same time. Introduce the use of three rhythms, then add in counting in 5s, using ig-u-an-o-don as the word. Photocopiable page 116 contains a visual representation of how the iguanodon rhythm fits in. This can be used as a visual aid, with children or adults pointing to the relevant line of rhythms, or left in the music corner for the children to use if they wish to practise with a friend.

Suggestion(s) for support

Stand any children who find the rhythms hard next to others who are confident. If the whole class finds it hard, go back to counting the 1-2-3-4 together, then build up to only shouting out the '1'. Alternatively, record the four-beat rhythm and clap the three-beat rhythm with the whole class while the tape is playing.

Assessment opportunities

This activity provides opportunities to monitor the children's awareness of multiple rhythms and their ability to keep a beat both together and independently of others.

Opportunities for IT

The children could use an art or drawing package to create a copy of the rhythm. If they use different symbols or colours for the two rhythms they will be able to see where the pulses for the two rhythms coincide.

The children could also use a word processor to write out the two words used in such a way that they can see the pattern of the rhythm emerging. Different colours could be used for each word or where the pulse comes for each of the rhythms.

```
CAT er pil lar   CAT er pil lar
BUT ter fly   BUT ter fly   BUT ter fly
```

This activity would also introduce the children to the idea of TABs to line up each of the parts of the rhythm, thus making it easier to follow. The children could go on to experiment with other words which have different rhythms, for example:

```
BE atle  or  HIPP o pot a mus.
```

Similar activities could be undertaken using framework software such as *My World 2* with the Musical Minibeasts file.

Display ideas

Ask the children to write out the rhythms on squared paper, showing where the first beat of the different rhythms coincide. By doing this the mathematics of the activity will be highlighted. This could also be done using a computer (see above). Alternatively, make a large frieze with cut-out pictures of caterpillars, butterflies and iguanodons so that the class can see how the sounds work together.

Reference to photocopiable sheets

Pages 115 and 116 provide pictures of the animals on a grid drawn in the correct position according to the number of beats in each name.

Moving forward

This activity makes an excellent introduction to Key Stage 2 work. 'Join the band' (page 84) asks the children to play along with the rhythms of music as they listen to it. In 'Grid notation' (page 106) children are asked to play four rhythms at the same time.

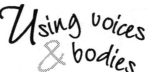

Decide on a subject or topic on which to base your musical word picture. It will help you to feel more confident if you have thought of a few descriptive words in advance. The theme of food has been chosen as the example here. Make a copy of photocopiable page 117, which gives examples of different ways to say 'greasy chips'.

Resources needed
Large sheets of paper for brainstorming words, copy of photocopiable page 117, pens, the Sunduza extract on the cassette, or any other music that uses voices alone to create sound effects.

What to do
Ask the children to tell you all their favourite foods, or animals, toys, drinks, games, and so on. Choose one, perhaps 'chips', and ask them to brainstorm all the words they can think of to do with that food. Ask them to think about:
▲ where they get chips;
▲ when they get them;
▲ what they smell like, taste like, sound like.

For chips you might end up with a list like yummy; hot; ketchup; chippy; greasy; yellow; fried; for tea; chip shop; and so on.

Choose just one of the words, perhaps 'greasy', and tell the children that you want them to think about all the different ways in which they could say that word. Ask them what sort of word it is:
▲ Is it a word that means something spiky and sudden, or is it smooth and drawn out?
▲ Is it a happy or sad word, boring or exciting?
▲ Are there any ways they can show this in the way they say the word?

Write down their ideas then, working as a whole class, say the word together in different ways.

You could start by saying it suddenly and quickly or in a long and drawn-out fashion

g...r...e...a...s...y...

or it could start softly and end on a loud note

gre**a**s**y**

or start on a high note and end on a low note

grea   sy

GREASY CHIPS

To develop children's experience of using words and voices as tools for composition.

†† *Whole class, then pairs.*

🕐 *30 minutes.*

♪ *Advanced.*

Previous skills/knowledge needed:
Several other activities lead into this one: 'Sounds in a circle' (page 28) is concerned mainly with developing timbre while 'Pitch dance' (page 34) deals with pitch. 'Rhythm and rhyme' (page 30) and 'The rhythm of story' (page 32) develop rhythmic skills, while 'Morning song' (page 35) explores the use of the voice. This whole range of skills will be useful in this activity, but are not essential.

Key background information
Using words as sounds is an ancient and powerful form of music-making. In India drumming rhythms are learned entirely by using voice sounds first. In African music words and voice are used very expressively, with imitations of many of the sounds heard in daily life – birds and animals, or mining picks and machines. Sunduza, a performance group from Zimbabwe, (extract 4 on the cassette which accompanies this book) create a highly effective train using voices only.

This activity concentrates on using the children's natural enthusiasm for creating everyday objects or situations to produce a piece that has atmosphere and a real feeling of whatever they are trying to create.

Vocabulary
Atmospheric, timbre, roaring, squealing, whispering.

Preparation
Listen to 'Isitimela Sangitshiya' by Sunduza. This will give you some idea of what can be done with voices, but is certainly not essential before carrying out the activity.

Explore the emphasis that is put on the different syllables. For instance, you could say **grea** sy or grea **sy**. In addition words can be whispered, roared or squeaked.

Before the class starts to say the word, set up a steady pulse. You can do this either with a quiet clap or by tapping on the carpet. Sometimes the word will last three or four pulses.

```
g r e a   sy   or   grea sy
1 2 3     4              1 2 3 4
```

Say the word in each style together as a class a few times, maintaining the pulse. When the children are confident, ask them to choose another word that they associate with chips from the list that they made at the beginning of the session. Do exactly the same thing with this word, trying to find as many ways as possible to say it. Give them time to experiment with a friend, emphasising that the reason they are doing this is to make the listener think straight away of chips when they hear the words spoken in these ways.

After five minutes stop the class and ask each pair to show what they have practised. If some children are shy about doing this ask them to show you, or another pair, and then have the whole class do it with them.

Explain to the class that they are going to put the piece together for a final showing, but before they do so play them the vocal music by Sunduza (extract 4 on the cassette) or your chosen music.

Discuss with the class how the piece should be put together. Ask questions:
▲ Do they want to start loudly or softly?
▲ Should everyone speak together?
▲ Do they want to start with one group by itself?
▲ How many times is the group going to say each word?
▲ How will they know when to start and stop?

Asking questions like these can often help to sort out agreement on how to perform the end piece.

Suggestion(s) for extension

Children who work through the activity confidently could be asked to work with a partner, with each person using a different word. Encourage them to think about how they will perform it:
▲ one speaking after the other;
▲ both speaking at the same time;
▲ using a mixture of the two methods;

▲ adding a movement with their sound;
▲ building up a moving pattern as they say their words.

Suggestion(s) for support

If some children find it hard to think up ways of saying new words, ask them to pick their favourite way of saying the original 'greasy' and say that in the circle.

If children are shy of talking in front of the group, put them with a large group. Often this is surprisingly non-threatening to children who have little confidence.

Assessment opportunities

Take this opportunity to observe the children's skill in using words and voices for composing.

Opportunities for IT

The children could use an art or drawing package to show how the words can be said in different ways. Some packages will allow children to bend, twist, squeeze or pull out words to make shapes which will emphasise the ways in which the words are said.

Most word processors will also allow children to experiment with different fonts and sizes to create similar effects. They will need to know how to change individual letters of a word and might like to use colour to emphasise particular sounds.

Display ideas

Think about the words that are being spoken in different ways and represent them artistically in different ways too, such as g r e a s y. Photocopiable page 117 provides some ideas.

This idea can be developed further to include representing the words in different colours and writing styles, expressed either by art work or computer graphics.

Reference to photocopiable sheet

Page 117 gives examples of ways in which words can be said, represented in a way that suggests how they would sound. It can be used as a stimulus within the lesson, and as a reference for the children's drawings of the words, as well as a basis for display.

Moving forward

This activity makes an excellent introduction to Key Stage 2 work. The use of voices can be extended into activities on composition, for example 'Making waves' (page 74) could use voices.

Using instruments

This chapter is as much about raising teachers' confidence with instruments as it is about developing children's skills. Teachers' natural fear of uncontrolled noise can easily result in a class of frustrated children spending twenty-eight minutes of a thirty-minute music lesson waiting for their turn to play a single instrument.

Children need to know that their teacher has very clear expectations about how they will handle instruments and when they will start, stop, play and listen, but they also need to know that they will be given plenty of opportunities to play.

This chapter builds on the routines and ground rules for working with instruments established in the *Basic skills* chapter (page 13), and uses them as starting points for further exploration. The wider the range of instruments you use (bought and class-made) and the more explorations you try, the more discoveries you and your pupils will make. You can return to any of these activities again and again as the children develop further skills in listening, playing and composing.

ADVENTURES IN SOUND

To develop children's awareness of timbre and confidence in using instruments.

†† *Whole class.*

⏱ *20 minutes.*

♫ *Easy.*

Previous skills/knowledge needed

It will be helpful if the children have had a chance to handle instruments before they try this activity. 'Starting and stopping' (page 14), 'Louder and softer' (page 20) and 'How does it sound?' (page 23) would all provide useful background experience.

Key background information

One view of music teaching holds that children should only be allowed to use instruments if they play them 'properly': that is, in the standard or conventional way. This activity moves away from that view, encouraging children to find as many different ways as they can to make sounds with any instrument. This experience will help them to understand how similar instruments are used in different types of music and in different parts of the world, as well as developing their confidence in handling them.

By exploring and combining instrumental sounds, they are finding out about timbre (quality of sound), texture (layers of sound) and structure (the way in which a sequence of sounds is put together). They are also learning to use dynamics (loud and quiet) as a way of experimenting with sounds.

Vocabulary

Instrument (and instrument names); loud, quiet, tap, shake, rattle, rub, scratch, and so on.

Preparation

Listen to the extract from *Orchestra of the forest* by Ray Lema on the cassette (or to your own selected music), focusing on the combination of sounds.

Resources needed

Enough instruments for the whole class to have one each (drums, tambourines, triangles, xylophones, and so on), cassette player, recording of *Orchestra of the forest* on the cassette which accompanies this book, or any other experimental music which explores instrumental sounds.

What to do

Sit the children in a circle and hand each one an instrument *silently*. Make sure the different types of instruments are well spread out around the circle. Using a signal for start and stop (see 'Starting and stopping' page 14) let them all try out their instruments at the same time: it will make a terrible noise, but if you don't let this happen, you are likely to have a class full of frustrated children for the next twenty minutes. Each time you stop them, praise them for responding to your signal, then invite them to try a new sound on the same instrument (a triangle, for example, sounds completely different when it is held tightly or loosely). Encourage the children to be as adventurous as they like in discovering new sounds: can they think of ways of playing their instruments that no-one else might have thought of?

After two or three minutes ask the children to pass their instruments one place around the circle and to repeat the experimentation with their new instruments, but this time ask them to explore very quiet sounds and then to contrast these, at your signal, with very loud sounds.

Discuss very briefly the kinds of sounds they have been making and how they produced them: ask two or three children to explain and demonstrate what they have been doing. You might point out that it is easier to hear the interesting sounds the different instruments are making when everyone is playing quietly than when everyone is playing loudly. (Remember that in this activity, volume is only a *vehicle* for exploring sounds: the object of the exercise is not simply to make loud and quiet sounds, but to discover how many *different* sounds can be made with one instrument.)

Ask the children to pass the instruments on again, give them one minute to explore different types of sounds at your request (perhaps rattling, rubbing or tapping) with their new instruments, then stop them. Explain that you are now going to put your sounds together to create a *musical structure*.

Point to each child in turn around the circle, asking them to start making a *scratching* sound on their instrument and to keep making it until you point to them again. As your hand passes round the circle a second time, each child stops in turn. Repeat this, asking the children to listen carefully to the combination of sounds they are making.

Now do the same with *banging* sounds, again passing your hand once around the circle to start each child, and a second time to stop them. Ask the children to listen carefully as they play.

Finally, select a number of children, asking them to play their most interesting sound continuously until you stop them. Be aware of the sounds you are combining in this way, and again ask the children to listen to the effect.

Now play the recording of *Orchestra of the forest* (or your own choice of music recording) and ask the children to describe the sounds they can hear. (The recording combines instrument sounds and animal noises.) Talk to the children about the way the different sounds contrast with each other, and the way in which one rhythm, in particular, is repeated against the background of other sounds.

Now choose a child as a conductor, and ask her to select sounds for the instruments to play (scratching, banging, rattling, shaking, tapping, and so on) and to start and stop them, either by pointing around the circle or by selecting individuals and signalling to them. Do this with two or three different conductors, then decide with the class on a structure for a final performance: you will need to discuss how you will start and finish your piece, as well as the types of sounds you want to use. Having heard the Ray Lema piece the children may choose to incorporate voice sounds, as well as instruments, into their composition.

Finally, perform your piece together, conducting yourself or asking a child to do so. Record the performance if possible, so the children can hear the effect when they do not have to concentrate on playing. You can then compare this recording with *Orchestra of the forest*, and discuss similarities and differences.

When you have carried out this activity several times, you may like to consolidate what the children have learned by writing, or asking them to write, descriptions of instrument sounds inside pictures of the instruments they have used. This will help the children to build up a vocabulary for describing timbre.

Suggestion(s) for extension

Children who have shown sensitivity and control in exploring instrument sounds will be ready to create their own compositions in a small group. They may want to take it in turns to conduct, but they should all be involved in making decisions about the types of sounds used and the overall structure of the piece.

A particularly challenging task is to create a composition using only quiet sounds and silence. This demands a high degree of attention, both from players and audience, but can be extremely effective and very rewarding.

Suggestion(s) for support

As with many activities, one of the most successful ways of supporting children who are experiencing difficulties is to put them in control. Many children lack confidence in exploring instrument sounds because they are not aware of the range of possibilities, so making decisions about how their classmates should play helps them to develop this awareness, as well as increasing their confidence.

Children who have difficulties with motor control need to learn what different ways of playing actually feel like. It will

help if you guide their hands to make different sounds at first, then give them some time to practise on their own.

Assessment opportunities

This activity enables you to gauge children's confidence in using instruments, their awareness of timbre, and their sensitivity to their own and each other's sound-making.

Opportunities for IT

Sounds made with a computer or keyboard can be explored in a similar way to those made with other instruments, except that the change in timbre is brought about by pressing a different key rather than by using a different movement or touch. Children who have shown a sensitivity to timbre could experiment with matching or comparing the timbres of electronic sounds with those of acoustic instruments. Children could use a word processor to present the words which describe the sounds made by their instrument. They could include pictures of the instrument, either drawn using an art package or taken from a collection of clip art.

Display ideas

Photographs of the children playing instruments can be displayed alongside their pictures and descriptions of instrument sounds. You could also create a 'sound forest' display using the Ray Lema piece to inspire drawings or paintings of a forest and combining these with pictures of instruments.

Moving forward

This activity links well with 'Something for nothing' (on this page), while 'Sounds in a circle' (page 28) explores voice sounds in a similar way. This activity also links particularly well with 'Building a sound house' (page 64), which focuses on timbre in order to build a sound picture.

SOMETHING FOR NOTHING

To enable the children to discover how to use everyday objects as musical instruments.

Session One: groups of four to five.
Session Two: whole class.
Session One: 15 minutes.
Session Two: 20 minutes.
Session One: easy.
Session Two: medium.

Previous skills/knowledge needed

It will help if the children have had some experience in controlling and exploring instrument sounds and working with rhythms before they try this activity. 'How does it sound?' (page 23), 'Copy and echo' (page 19) and 'Adventures in sound' (page 44) would all be useful for this.

Key background information

The use of non-musical equipment for making music in this activity is a deliberate challenge to the idea that music can only be made with purpose-built instruments. Across the world, from Africa to Latin America, and Europe, people – especially the poorest people – have been making music for centuries with whatever comes to hand. Whether in a street band or a classroom, nobody should ever be prevented from making music for lack of the right equipment. In 'Sounds in a circle' (page 28) and 'Rhythm and rhyme' (page 30) children are encouraged to explore voice and body sounds musically. This activity investigates ways of doing the same with the sounds of objects which can be found in any infant classroom, and uses an example from the contemporary composer John Cage to demonstrate how everyday sounds can be turned to a musical purpose.

The activity works best if you carry out your initial explorations with groups of four or five children at a time, but it would also be possible to teach both Session One and Session Two to the whole class. If you are working with just one group at a time, the other groups could be involved in independent musical activities: perhaps 'Composition cards' (page 69), 'Show time' (page 72) or 'Music corner cards' (page 103).

Vocabulary
Sound, loud, quiet, shake, rub, rattle, tap, and so on.

Preparation
Spend a little time exploring the sound-making potential of some of the ordinary objects in your classroom. For example, try out the sounds you can make by tapping your fingers on tables, chairs and books, shuffling shoes on hard floor and carpet, clicking pieces of construction or counting equipment

What to do
Session One
Working with a group of four or five children, ask them to see how many different sounds they can make with the things around them. Stress that they are to do this without moving from where they are. Try out some sounds yourself at the same time, to show the children that they really are free to experiment.

Talk to the children about the sounds they have made, and how they were produced – by rubbing, banging, tapping, and so on. Ask them to demonstrate some of their sounds, and to describe how they have made them. Play a call-and-response game with them, in which individuals 'play' rhythms for everyone else to copy.

If it proves difficult to think of rhythmic patterns for the others to copy, try simple phrases or song-lines (perhaps Baa baa black sheep, or One-a-penny, two-a-penny) beating these out while you say them in your head. (See 'Rhythm

together, or making up rhythm patterns on the computer keyboard. If you are working with individual groups for Session One, prepare activities for the rest of the class.

Before you undertake Session Two, listen to the recording of *Imaginary Landscape No. 2 (1942)* by John Cage. Focus on the kinds of sounds he uses and consider how you might produce similar sounds in the classroom. Alternatively, you can use a recording of any piece of music which incorporates the sounds of everyday objects.

Resources needed
For Session One: Anything and everything! There are no specified resources required for this activity: you simply use what is around you in the classroom.
For Session Two: Recording of *Imaginary Landscape No. 2 (1942)* by John Cage (or your own choice of music – see 'Preparation'), cassette player and blank cassette (optional).

and rhyme' (page 30) for an elaboration on this idea.) Encourage the children to try out as many different sounds as possible during this game.

Now explain to the children that you want them to try to see everything around them as musical instruments: the floor, the tables and chairs, all the equipment in the classroom. (You may rule out certain items here if you need to protect them from misuse.) Ask them to do a five-minute 'sound trek' around the classroom, trying out different sounds with different objects. After five minutes, ask them to bring their favourite sound-maker back to the area where you were working together – if someone has chosen a fixed object, such as a radiator or door, ask the rest of the group to gather round it with their sound-makers.

Select a sound-maker for yourself and repeat the call-and-response game, varying it by asking individuals or pairs to respond to your patterns rather than the whole group.

Finally, ask the children to take turns to play patterns for the rest of the group to copy. Point out that they must remember what their sound-maker is, as they will be using it for a whole-class performance when all the groups have carried out their initial investigations.

Session Two

When you have completed Session One with every group, bring the whole class together and discuss what everyone has done. Ask a few children to demonstrate their sounds, and to describe their sound-makers to the rest of the class.

Now play the recording of the piece by John Cage (or your chosen alternative). Ask the children to guess which objects are being used to make the sounds they can hear. Listen to the recording again, and ask the children to put up their hands each time they hear a different instrument or sound-maker coming in.

Ask the children to position themselves around the classroom with the sound-maker they chose during their group work. Those who are using fixed objects will need to be in specific places, but you can group all the other children together at tables or on the carpet. You can now use your improvised instruments for any number of simple musical activities:

▲ repeat the call-and-response game from Session One;
▲ tap out the rhythms of favourite songs or nursery rhymes, see 'Rhythm and rhyme' (page 30);
▲ experiment with combining different sounds without a fixed rhythmic pattern as in the John Cage piece.

You may want to repeat this session several times to explore different possibilities, and to record and compare the results.

Suggestion(s) for extension

Children who have shown imagination and ability in this activity can work in small groups to create their own 'found sound' compositions.

Suggestion(s) for support

Children who are unsure of how to respond to this activity may need help in finding things to play and exploring ways of playing them. Others may have difficulty copying rhythmic patterns: these children will benefit from working alongside those who are more confident with rhythms.

Assessment opportunities

This activity presents opportunities to assess children's awareness of how sounds are produced, their ability to use everyday objects as instruments and to play in time with the rest of the group or class.

Opportunities for IT

The children could use multimedia authoring software to link a picture of the object used to make the sound with a recording of the sound itself. The pictures could be drawn using an art or drawing package, scanned from children's own line drawings or taken from a clip art collection. The sound can be recorded using a microphone linked to the computer with suitable software.

Display ideas

Display pictures of the different 'instruments', or photographs of the children playing them, accompanied by descriptions of the sounds they make.

Moving forward

Improvised instruments can be used successfully in any of the rhythmic activities which follow this one. They would be particularly appropriate for 'Percussion band' (page 52) and 'Mini orchestra' (page 55), and for the percussion accompaniment to 'Multibeat' (page 38). They can also be a useful resource for children's own compositions (they might be particularly appropriate for 'Building a sound house' on page 64).

I shuffled my feet on the floor.

Daniel shook a tray of cubes.

'I liked it when Miss poured water down the sink.'

PASS THE BEATER

To develop children's confidence in using tuned percussion instruments and their awareness of melodic shape.

✝✝ *Whole class, working in groups of three.*

🕐 *20 minutes (though the activity could be split into two or more 15-minute sessions).*

🎵 *Easy.*

Previous skills/knowledge needed

Some experience in using and exploring instruments would be valuable. 'Copy and echo' (page 19) gives experience in copying rhythm, as does 'Adventures in sound' (page 44).

Key background information

This activity is designed to help children feel at ease with *tuned* percussion (such as xylophones, glockenspiels, metallophones, chime bars) and to give them experience of copying and being copied by others in a simple musical activity. The control passes from child to child, so everyone has a chance to feel what it is like to be in charge.

This activity differs from those with *untuned* percussion (such as 'Copy and echo' on page 19) in that the children are encouraged to copy the *shape* of the melody as well as its rhythm. For this reason, instruments such as xylophones are particularly appropriate for this activity, as the movement of the beater creates a shape in the air as it plays a tune.

This also works well on steel pans, so if you have an opportunity to use them, this activity would provide a good introduction.

Vocabulary

Xylophone, glockenspiel, metallophone, chime bar, beater, pattern, rhythm.

Preparation

Prepare the instruments. If you are using chime bars put them into sets of three or four, arranged in order of size with the largest (the lowest note) on the left. Each set will then count as one instrument. Practise a few simple tunes on the xylophones yourself, and notice the patterns that the beaters make as you play.

Resources needed

Enough tuned percussion instruments and beaters for the children to share one between three, with one extra for the teacher.

What to do

Seat the children in a circle, and give out one instrument (or a set of chime bars) and one beater to the first child of every group of three, keeping an instrument and beater for yourself. Play a simple pattern on your instrument, perhaps the one you practised earlier, using several notes so that the beater creates a shape in the air as you play.

For example you might play C D E F G F E D C

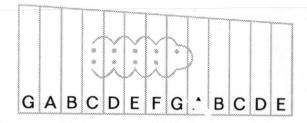

or C E G C G E C

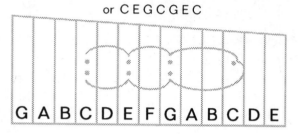

Ask the children who are holding the beaters to copy the pattern, all playing at the same time (they will probably not copy accurately, and they certainly won't play in time with each other, but this is not a problem, as the main purpose here is to give everyone an opportunity to play during the first few minutes).

When they have copied your pattern, ask the children to pass the beater to the second person in their group, then play a new pattern for these children to copy. Do the same for the remaining children so that everyone has had a turn at playing, then go round the groups once more, playing a new pattern each time. Ask the children to listen carefully and make their own tunes as much like yours as they can. Draw attention to the pattern that the beater makes as it plays: can the children make the same patterns with their beaters? Do their tunes sound like yours?

Now that you have demonstrated the idea of making patterns, you can hand over control to the children. Ask a few children to take it in turns to play a tune for *you* to copy. You will find that they gain great satisfaction from this: not only are they in control, but they can only be right and *you* can be wrong!

Each time you copy a pattern, ask the rest of the class whether you got it right, and if not, why not. This not only holds their attention while they are not playing but helps them develop a vocabulary for describing musical patterns. For example they might say:

▲ 'You went too high';

▲ 'Your notes were too spread out';

or they might focus on the rhythm rather than the melody, saying:

▲ 'You played too slowly';

▲ 'He went dum di dum, but you went dum, dum, dum'.

The children will find it easier to describe differences than to describe similarities, so it is worth getting it wrong a few times on purpose.

Continue with this until you have copied as many children in the class as you judge to be appropriate within one session. The children may remain involved and concentrate well while every member of the class has a turn, or they may grow restless after only five or six people.

Explain to the children that they are now going to copy each other in pairs. They should imagine that there is a giant clock hand stretching right across the circle of children: each group of three children will be paired with the group sitting opposite. (If you have an uneven number of groups make yourself the partner of one whole group.) As the imaginary clock hand turns, a new pair will play, with one child copying the other.

Starting with group A, the first child in the group plays a pattern which the first child in the opposite group copies. Then the second child in group A plays and the second in the opposite group copies, and so on all the way round the circle. (You might like to use a metre rule as your clock hand, to help the children see who their partners are and who is playing next.)

Everyone will have a chance both to lead and copy as the first child in the first group takes over as leader from the last child in the final group.

As soon as each child has played, he must pass his beater to the next person in the group, so that the tunes and echoes form a continuous pattern. The more often you do this activity, the more this will sound like a structured piece of music. Once the children are experienced at this, you can conclude by giving a performance which incorporates patterns copied by individuals and by groups.

Suggestion(s) for extension
Children who are adept at both generating and copying tunes can work together to make a simple 'echoes' composition.

A series of four simple echoed patterns will make a very effective piece of music, especially if played without a break. If you sing *I hear thunder* to yourself you will hear what a good example it is of a piece in which each line is repeated (see 'Reading a song' on page 105).

Suggestion(s) for support
Some children will be very reticent about making up their own tunes. Suggest that they use only two or three notes which are either very close together or very far apart. Their confidence will increase as they hear their own pattern echoed by others.

Assessment opportunities
Watch the children carefully to assess their ability to listen attentively, memorise and repeat rhythmic patterns and to generate patterns of their own. You will also be able to monitor the children's confidence in handling instruments and in playing in front of the rest of the class.

Display ideas
A display related to this activity could show both the way the activity was organised, using a diagram like the one shown on page 50, and the visual patterns made by the beaters as the tunes were being played.

Moving forward
'Composition cards' (page 69) offers opportunities to develop melodic awareness. 'Reading a song' (page 105) investigates the repeated pattern of *I hear thunder*, This is shown in formal notation on photocopiable pages 144 and 145.

🎧 PERCUSSION BAND

To enable children to apply the instrumental skills they have learned.

†† *Whole class, in instrument groups.*

🕐 *45 minutes (or two or more shorter sessions).*

♫ *Medium.*

Previous skills/knowledge needed

The children will need to have had experience of using percussion instruments, and of playing together. 'Keeping the beat' (page 18) and 'Copy and echo' (page 19) would be useful for this, as would 'Cut-and-paste composing' (page 60) and 'Show time' (Games One and Two) on page 72, as well as any of the earlier activities in this chapter. 'Grid notation' (page 106) introduces the type of notation used here, but this activity can be used on its own to introduce the same principle.

Key background information

This activity focuses on the application of the rhythmic skills the children have learned, using grid notation to represent rhythms. It places a strong emphasis on keeping a steady beat, playing together and listening to each other. There are a number of stages in this activity so you might want to take it slowly and spread it over two or more sessions.

Vocabulary

Rhythm, beat, grid.

Preparation

Set out the instruments in groups (drums together, triangles together, and so on). Make three copies of sheets 118 and 119; cut them in half and stick them on to cards. Photocopy sheet 120 (enlarge it if possible) and stick it on to card too. Listen to the recording on the cassette of the *Reggae Samba* played by a group of 9- to 10-year-old children at Walkergate Junior School in Newcastle-upon-Tyne (or your own choice of music).

Resources needed

Cassette player, recording of *Reggae Samba* on the cassette (or any other rhythmic piece in which several rhythms are played at once), enough percussion instruments for the whole class (these can include tuned and untuned percussion, class-made and improvised instruments), copies of photocopiable pages 118–120 (see 'Preparation', above).

What to do

Sit the children in one large group facing you and start a steady clap of 1-2-3-4, with an emphasis on the first beat. Without stopping, invite the children to join in with the clapping. Tell them to keep in time with you as you gradually speed up and slow down: they will need to watch and listen very carefully to match their claps to yours.

Next, count a steady 1-2-3-4, only clapping on the first beat, but counting all the time. Ask the children to join in with you. (If they have tried 'Multibeat' on page 38 they will be very familiar with this.)

Now show the children rhythm card 1 from photocopiable page 118 and explain that this is one way of writing down what they have been clapping.

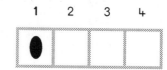

Ask the children to play the rhythm four times without stopping: remind them that they need to clap on the first beat each time, and count silently on beats 2, 3 and 4. Once they can do this confidently, introduce rhythm cards 2, 3 and 4 (number 4 is the hardest to clap). With each new rhythm, you can ask for volunteers to 'sight-read' the card, clapping the rhythm several times without stopping. Finally, show the children the whole grid on your final card which shows all four rhythms together.

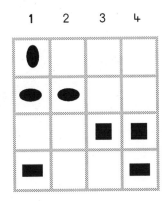

(For other ways of using a chart like this, see 'Grid notation' (on page 106).

Give out the instruments, with all the triangles, all the drums, and so on, together in groups. Allow the children two or three minutes for free experimentation on their instruments, then give one rhythm card to each group. (You will probably have more than one group playing the same rhythm.) Give them a few minutes to practise the rhythms on their cards, then ask each group to play their rhythm four times to the rest of the class. Now use the whole grid to conduct the entire class as they play their rhythms together, bringing the groups in one at a time. Keep the rhythms going for as long as you like, then stop all the groups, either at the same time, or one by one.

Play the recording of the *Reggae Samba* on the cassette (or your own choice of music) and ask the children to clap or tap along with it (they will probably do this spontaneously).

Encourage them to listen carefully to the way the rhythms go together. Tell them that the music on the tape is being performed by a class of 9- to 10-year-olds – they will probably be both astonished and encouraged!

Now ask the children to try their performance again, thinking about the way the children played in the recording. Keep practising (you can extend this over several sessions if you like, and listen to the recording a number of times). When your percussion band is ready, you can give a concert to another class, to parents or to the whole school (you might also play the *Reggae Samba* recording at your concert). If you record the performance, the children will have an opportunity to compare it with the recording and to see how well they match up.

Suggestion(s) for extension
Children who have shown the ability to repeat their rhythm accurately and to keep in time can devise their own rhythmic patterns, perhaps making up an entire new composition for the class percussion band to play. They could notate this using the blank grid on photocopiable page 147 (see 'Grid notation' on page 106).

Suggestion(s) for support
Children who have difficulty playing a rhythm against others may do better if they keep to the first pattern, playing only the first beat of every four. It will help if they count 1-2-3-4, 1-2-3-4 while they are playing.

Assessment opportunities
This activity will help you to note the children's ability to apply the instrumental skills they have learned, to memorise and repeat a simple rhythmic pattern, to play as a member of a group and to follow grid notation.

Opportunities for IT
The children could use a drawing package with a background notation grid on which they can record the rhythms using their own symbols. The grid could be set up in advance by

the teacher with a collection of appropriate symbols around the edge of the grid. The children could then copy the symbol and drag it to the appropriate place on the grid to record their compositions. They could also drag the symbols into the different positions in order to rearrange the rhythmic patterns themselves.

Display ideas
The grid notation for this activity can be displayed, both as a full grid and as a set of separate lines, along with written explanations and descriptions of the instruments used and the skills developed.

Reference to photocopiable sheets
Photocopiable pages 118 and 119 give the four separate rhythms used in this activity, while photocopiable page 120 shows all four rhythms together on a whole grid, which can be used to conduct the whole class. The blank grid on photocopiable page 147 can also be used for extension work.

Moving forward
This activity provides a good preparation for 'Mini orchestra' (page 55), as well as developing the essential skills of playing rhythmic patterns and keeping in time, which will form a useful basis for many of the activities in the *Composing* chapter (particularly Game Three of 'Show time' on page 72). The use of grid notation will also enable children to record their own compositions, as well as reading those composed by others (see 'Grid notation' on page 106).

🎧 MINI ORCHESTRA

To help the children to apply the instrumental skills they have learned and to appraise their own and each others' performances.

†† *Session One: whole class and instrumental groups.*
Session Two: whole class.
Session Three: whole class, then groups of three to five.

🕐 *Three 40-minute sessions.*

🎵 *Advanced.*

Previous skills/knowledge needed

This activity draws on all the instrumental and rhythmic skills developed in this chapter, and makes use of all available instrumental resources. Most of the activities in this chapter are relevant here, and the following activities from a range of chapters would be particularly useful as a preparation: 'Rhythm and rhyme' (page 30) and 'Percussion band' (page 52) for developing rhythmic skills while 'Pass the beater' (page 49) helps children to develop an awareness of melodic patterns. 'Join the band' (page 84) would be useful preparation for this activity, as it uses the same technique of joining with a recording as is used here. For Session Three, the children will need to have some experience of using informal notation (the activity 'Graphic notation' (page 100) could be helpful for this). If you do not feel confident about notation it is possible to complete Sessions One and Two without Session Three.

Key background information

One of the difficulties inherent in primary music is that it is very hard to make the sounds produced in the classroom sound anything like the sounds children associate with music in the real world. However hard you try, you cannot make thirty 7-year-olds sound like a symphony orchestra! However, it *is* possible to find examples of music from the real world, particularly from contemporary music, which have a lot in common with the sort of music children *can* create in the classroom, and to use these as a link between the two. This activity aims to do this, by providing, as a stimulus, a composition which combines jazz saxophone and traditional West African rhythms. This music is on the cassette which accompanies the book, but you could use any other piece of rhythmic, patterned music with a high degree of repetition.

Vocabulary

Rhythm, orchestra, instruments (and instrument names), notes.

Preparation

Listen to the recording of *Soli* by Sékou Camara Cobra on the cassette or to your own selection of music, paying particular attention to the rhythm of the music and the way in which the instruments are used. Make a copy of photocopiable page 121 for each child.

Resources needed

For all sessions: Recording of *Soli* by Sékou Camara Cobra (extract 8 on the cassette) or your own choice of rhythmic music, cassette player, a blank cassette (optional), a combination of tuned and untuned instruments – enough for the whole class and one for yourself (incorporating class-made and improvised instruments as well as bought ones if you like).

rhythms being played at once, so they may choose to tap the simplest, or to try one of the more complex patterns.) Talk to the children about the way that the saxophone weaves a tune above the rhythmic sound of the drums. Give out the instruments, grouping all instruments of the same type together. Give the children (and yourself) a couple of minutes to experiment with the instruments, then stop them and ask them to join in with the music quietly on their instruments while you play the same section of the recording again. (Join in with your own instrument too.) The children do not need to play anything complex: they just need to keep in time with the music. Select two or three children who have grasped the rhythm to demonstrate to the class while you play the recording a third time.

Split the class into the different instrumental groups and ask each group to work out a rhythm to play in time with the recorded music. It doesn't matter whether they are playing tuned or untuned instruments at this point: they simply need to use their instruments to create a rhythm. Play the recording a couple of times while they are practising, so that they can make sure that what they do fits with the music. Give the children about ten minutes to practise and develop their rhythms and tunes, then bring them back together. Ask each group to demonstrate what they have been doing, then ask the whole class orchestra to play their parts along with the recording. You can try this both in unison (with everyone playing together) and with different groups playing at different times. Ask the children to listen carefully to the other groups when they are not playing themselves. Conclude the session by asking the children to comment on their own and each other's performances, and to suggest ways in which they might be improved.

Session Two

Start this session by reminding the children about the rhythms and tunes they created for their instrumental groups in Session One. Play the recording of *Soli* and ask them to play along with it as before, but this time *fade the recording out after the first half minute or so*, and let the children carry on playing on their own. Talk to the children about what the combination of rhythms sounded like, and how they might improve it. At this point some of the children might suggest that they could use the tuned instruments to play tunes instead of rhythms – if not, you may need to suggest this yourself. Either way, pair each group playing tuned instruments up with one or more groups playing untuned instruments, and ask them to work together on a combined rhythm and tune to go with the recorded music. (The tune can be as simple as they like: all the players in the group can play the same notes, or they might combine different notes to create harmonies.) As before, play the recording once or twice while they are working, so that they can fit their compositions to the recording. After about ten minutes, bring the groups back together to demonstrate their rhythm and

Session Two: Large sheet of paper, felt-tipped pens, writing materials, copy of photocopiable page 153 (My performance) for each child.

Session Three: The whole-class performance plan written in Session Two, plain paper and writing materials for each group of three to five children.

What to do
Session One

Ask the children what they know about orchestras:

▲ What kinds of instruments do they have in them?

▲ What sorts of music do they play?

The children may well be familiar with orchestral playing in cartoon and film scores and popular classics: some of them may have learned about orchestral instruments in cartoons about Oscar the piano. Tell them that an orchestra can be any collection of instruments: for example, a Gamelan orchestra from Indonesia is a collection of gongs, metallophones and drums. The children's own orchestra will consist of all the instruments available to them as a class.

Play the recording of *Soli* to the children, asking them to listen at first, then tap their hands on their knees in time with the rhythm as the music continues. (There are actually several

tunes to each other then work with the whole class together to plan a performance of their combined pieces, incorporating both small group and whole-class playing. (The latter might be a combination of all the groups together, or you could return to the whole-class rhythms used in Session One. Write a performance plan (using words, symbols or a combination of the two) on a large sheet of paper.

When you have written it down, play through the piece twice without stopping. Discuss what it sounded like and how it might be improved. Note down any changes you wish to make on your performance plan, then invite volunteers to take over from you as the conductor. Each conductor can lead the class through the piece, then comment on the orchestra's performance. (You can become a member of the orchestra yourself at this point.) Repeat this as many times as you wish and consider recording and listening to the performance at this point, so that the children can hear what they sound like.

Conclude this session by asking each child to complete an evaluation sheet (photocopiable page 153), commenting on his own performance. They can also add an evaluation of the performance of the whole class orchestra, or an evaluation of their own group's composition, using photocopiable page 152.

Session Three

Start this session by listening to the recording of *Soli* and to the recording (if you made one) of the last session's whole-class performance. Ask the children to describe how the music was put together:

▲ Did different instruments play at different times?

▲ Was the same rhythm or tune played on different instruments?

Remind the children of the difference between the beginning, the middle and the end of the piece.

Now look together at the whole-class performance plan from Session Two, and discuss how this was structured. Ask the children to imagine that they are all composers, and that they have been commissioned to write a composition for their own class orchestra. Divide the class into groups of three to five (these can be different from the instrumental groups) and give each group several sheets of plain paper and some writing materials. Tell them that they can work out rhythms and patterns using hands and voices, but that they will not be able to hear what their composition really sounds like until it is played by the whole orchestra. The groups can write down their compositions in any way they choose (this will depend on how much experience they have had of experimenting with notation), the one essential requirement is that they must be able to explain what their symbols mean to the rest of the class. Remind the groups that their composition must include every instrument in the class orchestra.

Give the groups about 20 minutes to work on their compositions, then bring the orchestra together to try out each group's work. The members of each group will be responsible for explaining and conducting their own compositions, and for evaluating the orchestra's performance of their work. (You may like to extend this process over several sessions, with each group revising its composition a number of times.)

When the groups are satisfied with their compositions

and performances, they can give a grand concert to another class or the rest of the school. They can also record their pieces and keep the recordings in the classroom music corner (as this activity draws on so many different skills, a recording of this sort would be a good summary example of the children's work).

Suggestion(s) for extension

Children who have worked confidently on this task can be invited to compose more highly-structured melodies for the tuned instruments to play, with a rhythmic backing for the untuned instruments.

Suggestions(s) for support

This activity will be very challenging for some children, in both the playing and composing elements. It will help if they play untuned rather than tuned instruments in the first two sessions. In the third session they should work with more confident children to see how decisions are made in putting a piece of music together.

Assessment opportunities

The first two sessions of this activity provide opportunities to assess children's ability to listen carefully, to memorise and copy a rhythmic pattern, to keep in time and to play as members of a group. They will also use these skills in the third session as well as the ability to contribute ideas for a group composition and to lead others in a performance. All three sessions require the children to apply the instrumental skills they have learned, to evaluate their own and each others' performances, and to talk about the recorded music that they hear.

Opportunities for IT

The children could set up a grid notation system and drag symbols from a selection prepared by the teacher and set around the edge of the grid or they could create their own

graphic notation system (see 'Graphic notation' on page 100 or 'Grid notation' on page 106). They could also use a drawing package to present their final score.

The children could also use commercial software such as Topologika's *Music Box* to create their own score.

Display ideas

Pictures of orchestras or other musical groups can be displayed with the children's evaluations of their own performance. The whole-class composition and the group compositions can be displayed beside a description of the composition process and evaluations of the results.

Reference to photocopiable sheets

Photocopiable page 121 (Instruments of the orchestra) should provide useful stimulus throughout. Photocopiable page 152 (My composition), invites children to focus on their composition skills. Photocopiable page 153 (My performance) is an evaluation sheet for children to appraise their performance.

Moving forward

The children can apply the skills developed in this activity to composition work. 'Composition cards' (page 69), 'Show time' (page 72) and 'Making waves' (page 74) would provide opportunities for this. This activity also provides a good introduction to work at Key Stage 2.

Composing

Composing is about making choices: choices about sounds, patterns, rhythms, or notes, and choices about the way and the order in which they are played. It is about choosing and combining sounds for a purpose: to produce an effect, to stir an emotion, to create an atmosphere. Whether you are composing for a symphony orchestra, a triangle or a range of body sounds, these decisions still have to be made.

Teachers often worry about tackling composing with their pupils because they are unsure of how to start them off, what to ask them to do and how to respond to them when they have done it. The activities in this chapter address all these issues, using a range of different themes and starting-points and drawing on the children's developing skills in all areas of music (links with activities in other chapters are given).

The key to success in these activities is believing in what the children are doing and treating them as composers right from the start. If you believe that the five-year-old's single 'ping' on a triangle is a composition, she will believe it too. From this point, anything can happen!

CUT-AND-PASTE COMPOSING

To introduce and develop the concept of playing a sound from reading a symbol.

†† *Groups of four or five, possibly with adult support.*

🕐 *55 minutes.*

♪ *Easy.*

Previous skills/knowledge needed

Children may gain more from this activity if they have tried 'Starting and stopping' (page 14).

Key background information

Here the children will compose by choosing pictures that they like and at the end of the activity they will perform the piece they have composed. The realisation that a symbol can be used to represent sound can be developed later to show greater detail of how short, loud, or soft the sounds should be, but this is the first step.

Vocabulary

Names of the instruments on the two photocopiable sheets:
Page 122 – triangle, tambourine, drum, maracas/shakers, cymbal, guiro/scraper, glockenspiel;
Page 123 – tambour, cowbell, ago-go, bongo drums, temple bells, bells, xylophone.

Preparation

Photocopy a composition sheet (page 124) and instrument picture sheets (photocopiable pages 122 and 123) for every child trying the activity. Check that your school has all the instruments in the pictures. If you do not have a particular instrument, blank out its picture before you copy the sheet. Similarly, if you wish to use an instrument which is not pictured, draw it in the blank box on either sheet. Lay out all the instruments in a 'performance corner' – you should also prepare a corner where the children can stick down their pictures – this should not be too near the performance corner.

Resources needed

Adequate numbers of photocopied sheets, adhesive, scissors, instruments (see 'Preparation', above).

What to do

In the performance corner, show the children the sheet of instrument pictures. Depending on the age and experience of the children either offer the full choice of instruments or just the set on page 122.

Show the children the instruments, saying the name of each one. Play each instrument with a single bang or jingle, making it clear that the children will be playing them at the end of their activity. Move to the area set aside for sticking down and show the children the blank grid (page 124) on to which they will stick their pictures.

Ask the children to chose which instrument pictures they want to stick on to their grid – explain that only one picture will fit in each square on the grid. Let the children cut out the pictures and stick them in place, in their chosen order, on the grid. Tell the children that, at the moment, they are to play one jingle or bang for each time the picture is pasted on to the grid. As they grow more familiar with the activity they could decide for themselves how many bangs or jingles they want to make for each picture.

When their grids are complete, ask the children to take their 'music' over to the performance corner to practise in pairs. Explain that they should set out the instruments in the order in which they will be played, then take turns to be the player and pointer. The pointer points to the pictures on the grid in the correct order, reading from left to right, while the player plays the required instrument. Ask them to play each piece through four times without stopping. This will make it sound like a structured piece of music. When they have finished, the player and pointer swap.

When all the groups have practised they should give a performance in the performance corner to another group, the whole class, or other adults.

In response to the performance, draw attention to the positive points in individuals' performances:
▲ the concentration that Joanna had;
▲ the way Anwar kept his triangle quiet when it was supposed to be silent;

▲ the interesting pattern that Martin played on his bells.

In addition, it could provide a good opportunity to highlight the basics of notation.

Ask the children questions such as:

▲ How did you know which instrument to play first?

▲ Where does the music start/stop?

▲ How do you know which way up it should be?

▲ What instrument did you start with?

▲ Can you show where the drum is on the music?

▲ What would happen if I asked you to play it twice?

▲ Do you think twice sounds better than four times?

▲ How was Joanna's triangle playing different from Martin's triangle playing?

▲ Does the music tell you how long to play the triangle for?

The last questions lead on to considering more specific methods of notation (see the *Notation* chapter).

Suggestion(s) for extension

If the children find the activity easy, provide a longer grid and introduce the idea of having two instruments played within one square (at the same time). Alternatively, ask the children to make up a way to show how long to play for or what sound pattern to make. You could also ask a group of children to play one child's composition (using one instrument each).

Suggestion(s) for support

If the children struggle with the activity, restrict the number of instrument pictures, have pictures already cut out, or make the grid smaller.

Assessment opportunities

During performance is an ideal time to assess whether a child understands the concept of playing from symbols. It should also be possible to observe their motor skills while playing the instruments.

Opportunities for IT

The children could use a drawing package with an associated collection of musical instrument pictures to present and publish their final composition. If pictures of the instruments are placed around the drawing area (which could also contain a grid) the children can select an appropriate instrument, copy it and then drag it into position on the drawing area. This could be set up in advance by the teacher and saved, so that children can retrieve the starting file and then save it with their own filename. The same activity could be set up using framework software like *My World 2* with an appropriate instrument file set up by the teacher.

A more sophisticated approach would be to use a multimedia authoring package and link the pictures to the sounds made by the instrument so that the final tune can be played by clicking on the instruments. The sounds of the various instruments could be recorded using a microphone attached to the computer.

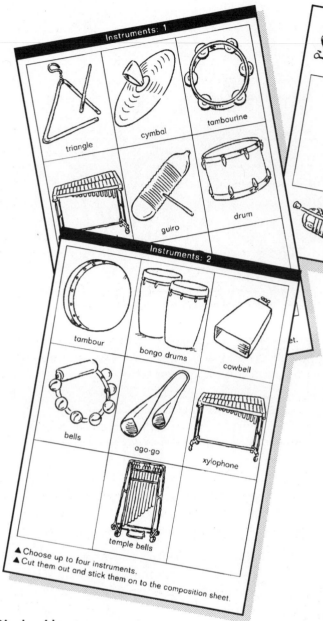

PATTERNS AND RHYTHMS

To introduce the idea of sequencing musical patterns as a form of composing.

†† *Whole class or groups of four to five.*

🕐 *40 minutes.*

♪ *Easy.*

Previous skills/knowledge needed

The children need to have had experience of playing to a steady pulse and also composing and playing simple rhythms. 'Copy and echo' (page 19) and 'Keeping the beat' (page 18) introduce and develop these skills.

Key background information

There is pattern and sequence in all music, whether it be pop, classical or heavy metal. Often the pattern is that of a very simple selection of notes or rhythms called a *motif*. This is repeated in sequences that may stay the same or vary. Giving the children opportunities to create their own rhythmic patterns and put them into a sequence will give them the vocabulary and experience to analyse or compose more complicated structures.

Vocabulary

Rhythm, pattern, sequence.

Preparation

Before the activity it might be useful to think up four rhythmic patterns, each lasting the space of four beats. If you can't think of any rhythms use a few phrases from a nursery rhyme as rhythm patterns, such as
▲ Baa baa black sheep;
▲ Humpty Dumpty sat on the wall;
▲ Mary Mary quite contrary.

Display ideas

Display the children's music and photographs of them performing in the performance corner. Invite other children to have a go at playing this music.

Reference to photocopiable sheets

Photocopiable pages 122 and 123 have pictures of instruments, with blank spaces on each sheet in which the teacher may draw any further instruments which will be used in the activity. Photocopiable page 124 is the Composition sheet on to which the children stick the pictures.

Moving forward

The children could develop their skill in reading from symbols in 'Grid notation' (page 106) and 'Percussion band' (page 52). This activity also links well with 'Adventures in sound' (page 44) in which the children are developing their awareness of timbre in instruments. 'Show time' (page 72) uses the concept of creating a composition using symbols.

What to do

Sit the children in a group where they can all see you. Tell them that you are going to perform a simple rhythm pattern. Ask them to watch you carefully and repeat the pattern when you have finished it. Play a simple pattern which lasts for four pulses or beats. You might do four slaps on your knees, or two slaps and two taps on your shoulders – even two claps and two silences. At the end of this pattern show, possibly by a nod of your head, that it is the children's turn to do the pattern. Introduce this first pattern as 'pattern one'. Continue the call and response of this pattern until the children are confident they know what pattern one is.

Now move on to pattern two. This pattern should also last for four pulses or beats but otherwise you can do whatever you wish. It doesn't need to be a more complex rhythm unless you feel that the children responded very quickly to the first rhythm and now need stretching a little. Consider eight fast claps, or two stamps followed by two nods of the head. Again do call and response with pattern two, as with pattern one, and then introduce pattern three.

Pattern three will also last for four pulses or beats. After practising pattern three till the children are confident with it, explain that you are now going to play a game in which you call out the number of one of the patterns and see whether the children can repeat that pattern. When the children are doing this confidently you could split them into smaller groups and let each group play the game with one of the children calling the number of the pattern.

As the children become more confident with this ask them, still working in their groups, to choose an order in which to play patterns one, two and three. Make it clear that they can choose any order they like. If you feel the children are ready for it, you could also introduce different conditions:

▲ they can play any pattern twice;
▲ they can play pattern one up to four times;
▲ the composition must always end with pattern three, and so on.

Give the children four or five minutes to practise their rhythm compositions, then ask them to perform for the whole group. Use this to emphasise the importance of a listening audience. Remind the children who are performing that they are in charge and should therefore not start their piece until their audience is silent. This attitude will help the children to take their own and other people's music seriously.

After each group has demonstrated its patterns, ask the children about what they have heard:

▲ Which pattern was played first?
▲ How many times was pattern one played?
▲ Which was the hardest pattern to play?

As a grand finale, play the pieces one after another, either in assembly or to another class. Alternatively, tape the whole piece so that the children can listen to it.

Suggestion(s) for extension

Children who find this easy could be asked to make up a pattern of their own and add this to their sequence.

Suggestion(s) for support

Children who find this activity difficult should be encouraged to participate fully in the group. This will support them and build up their confidence. They could also be given simpler patterns.

Assessment opportunities

While the children are practising and also while they are showing what they have done, there will be good opportunities to observe motor co-ordination, their ability to copy, remember and repeat a simple sequence, and their ability to keep a pulse going. It should also be possible to assess whether the children can memorise or use rhythmic pattern in composition, or sequence musical patterns.

Opportunities for IT

As an extension to this activity children could use a drawing package to create their own sequences of symbols to make their composition. They could use a set of symbols, such as squares, circles or triangles which are easy to produce on most drawing packages. These could also be coloured in.

It would be useful to have a background grid for this activity with the 'snap to grid' option turned on to help children line up the symbols. The composition could be printed out so the children could assign instruments to the symbols and play each others' music.

The children could use software like *Compose* or *Compose World* to create their own musical patterns and sequences.

Display ideas

Take photographs of the children working and display these alongside the children's descriptions of the sound patterns they made. Any computer printouts the children have produced could also be displayed.

Moving forward

'Heads and tails' (page 81) explores patterns in songs, while 'Percussion band' (page 52) and 'Grid notation' (page 106) make use of patterns to represent rhythmic patterns. 'Join the band' (page 84) enables children to join in with the rhythmic pattern of a song.

BUILDING A SOUND HOUSE

To develop children's ability to create atmosphere through sound effects.

†† *Whole class, working in small groups.*

🕐 *Two 30-minute sessions.*

♫ *Medium.*

Previous skills/knowledge needed

The children need to be aware of the type of sounds that can be created. 'How does it sound?' (page 23), 'Layers of sound' (page 25) and 'Adventures in sound' (page 44) would all provide good preparation for this activity.

Key background information

In order to compose music the children will require the skills of listening to, and being aware of, a range of sounds. They also need to be able to decide on an order in which to play those sounds, and a way to play them that creates a particular feeling or pattern, or just sounds pleasant.

Vocabulary

Gurgle, flush, splosh, splash, ring, hum, buzz, calm, happy, exciting, busy.

Preparation

Collect together and have ready a wide range of instruments or everyday articles for useful sound effects (or be prepared to have your class plundered!) Make copies of the 'furnished' and 'unfurnished' sound house (photocopiable pages 125 and 126), enough to have one for every group of five children.

Resources needed

One copy each of photocopiable pages 125 and 126 for each group of five children, instruments or artefacts for sound effects, pencils.

What to do

Session One

Seat the children where they can all see you. Show them one copy of the 'furnished' sound house (page 125) and explain the idea of making sound effects for the different appliances that are in the rooms. Now ask the children to shut their eyes and think of their favourite room in their own house. After a few seconds, ask them to open their eyes and ask one child to make a sound (using his voice or part of his body) that would give the rest of the class a clue to the room he was thinking of (perhaps the sound of a bubbling saucepan or the 'ping' of a microwave for a kitchen; an alarm clock for a bedroom). The child who guesses correctly has the next turn, and so on.

When the children are confident with this idea, divide the class into groups of four or five and give out one 'unfurnished' sound house sheet (page 126) to each group. Explain that

▲ Is it a repeated sound or one long sound?

▲ Does the bubbling water sound excited and jumpy or smooth and flowing?

Ask the children to decide which instrument or piece of classroom equipment (rulers, pencils, crayons rattled in pots, paper crunched, and so on) would mimic each sound effect. Using the 'furnished' sound house sheets as a stimulus, ask the children to work in their groups to create sound effects for either a single room or, eventually, a whole house.

Depending on the age, stage and experience of the class you might want to stipulate that they just do the sound effects for one room and decide, as they work, how much more it would be suitable to develop, or you could choose to do this as a one-off activity and ask each group to contribute one room to a complete house. Remind the children that they can use instruments, or artefacts from the classroom. You may also need to give out new 'unfurnished' sound house sheets so the groups can draw in the sound effects that they are making (or they may be continuing work on their sheets from the previous session).

Point out that they will have to decide whether they are going to play all the sounds at the same time or one after another. They also need to decide on an order for the sound effects and a way to record this on the sheet. Give the groups three or four minutes in which to practise, then stop them and tell them that they will be showing each other what they have done in another three minutes' time. By stopping the children you refocus their attention so that they concentrate in two separated three-minute chunks, rather than having their attention start to wander after four minutes.

Finally, bring all the children back together and say that they are going to have a grand performance. You could try to tape what they have done or arrange to show the rest of the school in assembly.

Suggestion(s) for extension

If the children have found this activity easy ask them if they can show, by the way they represent their sound effect, whether it is night or day, early in the morning or coming-home time, even a particular day of the week. Ask them to think about whether the sound effects would change with the seasons.

It would also be possible to link this with topic work – what would a house in a fairy story (perhaps *Sleeping Beauty*) be like?

Alternatively, ask the children to think about what would happen if they were walking out of one room and into another. Can they make one set of sounds fade out while another becomes gradually louder as they enter the new room?

Suggestion(s) for support

If the children are finding the activity difficult ask them to think of *one* sound in each room and then play the rooms in turn.

they will have five minutes to play the game in their groups. As each sound effect is made and guessed they should draw it in the appropriate room in the 'unfurnished' house.

After ten minutes, bring the children together again and ask each group to make a sound effect from one room of the house they have just created. Ask the rest of the class to guess which room the sound effect came from. You may have a wide range of rooms represented, or you may find that every group represents the kitchen – this does not matter, the important thing is that they understand the notion of representing something with a sound effect. This would be a suitable point at which to pause if you wish to do the activity in two sessions.

Session Two

Remind the children of the activity by discussing the sound effects that they would hear in each room. Lead the discussion towards the type of sounds that are being made by asking questions such as:

▲ Is the sound of the alarm clock high or low?

▲ Does the microwave 'ping' sound short or long?

Composing

Ask them to draw three things they might find in one of the rooms, decide what sounds they might make and choose three instruments to play the sounds.

Opportunities for IT

The children could use a keyboard to create their sound picture. Many keyboards have a range of synthesised sound effects which could be used, and on some keyboards it would be possible to tape-record the composition.

The children could also use a multimedia authoring package to create a sound picture of the house. Different groups could record the sound effects for different rooms in the house and the software could be set up so that clicking with the mouse on an item, such as the microwave, gives the sound effect for it. The sounds could be recorded using a microphone attached to the computer.

Display ideas

This idea of different sounds in different rooms in the house could be extended to work with descriptive words. Use these words and the sound house sheets to make a huge 'sound collage' of a house to hang on the wall.

Alternatively, label the home corner with indications of sounds which should be played in different areas.

Reference to photocopiable sheets

Photocopiable page 125 shows a 'furnished' sound house and is used by the children as a stimulus. Page 126 shows an 'unfurnished' house which can be used to record the children's compositions.

Moving forward

'Making waves' (page 74) develops further the use of sounds and atmosphere. 'Talking about music' (page 88) provides opportunities for children to talk about how other composers create atmosphere in their music.

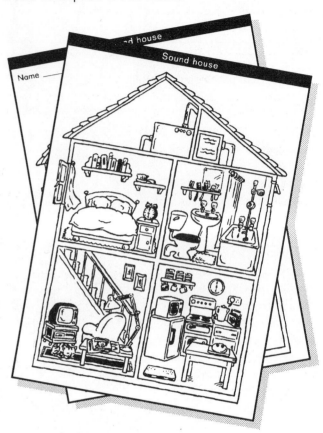

Composing

BATNOTES

To introduce the concept of composing a simple theme using a few notes.

†† *Individuals, groups of two or three, or whole class working in small groups, subject to resources.*

🕐 *40 minutes.*

🎵 *Medium.*

Previous skills/knowledge needed
The children would benefit from experience in using pitch and melody. 'Pitch dance' (page 34) provides awareness of the pitch of different notes, while 'Pass the beater' (page 49) gives awareness of melody.

Key background information
Many effective and famous tunes use only one or two notes for their main theme. The theme music for the *Jaws*, *James Bond* and *Batman* films and television series all use a strong insistent rhythm, and just a few notes, to create a very effective theme tune. As with any simple piece of music the result can be either electrifying or a complete flop – this will depend on the thought and commitment given to it by the performer.

Vocabulary
Tune, melody, theme, rhythm.

Preparation
Hum the theme tune of the Batman television series to yourself (dina, dina, dina, dina, dina, dina, dina, dina, Batman!) If you wish to use other music, choose a well-known theme tune that uses a few notes and a strong, simple rhythm. Find either three chime bars, C, B, A or remove bars from a glockenspiel or xylophone to give the same effect. (If you have a B flat that is even better as it is the actual note used. These are the black Bs.) Practise playing the Batman theme.

Resources needed
As many collections of the notes C, B, A, as you have. This can be in the form of recorders, penny whistles or keyboards as well as chime bars, glockenspiels and xylophones.

What to do
Play the theme tune of Batman to the children on your chime bars. Play it several times until they can sing it back to you. Ask them whether they recognise the music and know what it is the theme tune of. Discuss what the Batman story is about.

Then ask the children to listen to the music once again and tell you how many different notes are being used in the tune. There is generally some confusion between notes (in this case C, B, A) and how many times each note is played. The children will almost certainly count the number of times each note is played and tell you the grand total of 16!

It is worth spending a little time drawing attention to the difference between these two concepts. You can do this by using children to be the different notes. Ask one child to be the 'C', one child to be the 'B', and one child to be the 'A'. Every time their note is played they have to stand up. This will create some fast-moving standing up and sitting down but will also reinforce the point that a complex effect can be achieved using only three children (or notes).

Next, let the children learn to play the Batman theme. The tune and rhythm can best be described by saying:

> dinna, dinna, dinna, dinna,
> dinna, dinna, dinna, dinna,

with the final – BATMAN! – spoken or shouted.

```
C C  B B  A A  B B
C C  B B  A A  B B
```

If you are teaching the activity as a whole-class lesson you will now need to divide the class into groups of about four, each with a set of notes. Obviously the number of groups you have will depend on the number of resources available. Ask the groups of children to sit round their allocated instruments.

Give each child in the group a number – 1, 2, 3 or 4 and provide each group with just one beater. To learn to play the

tune the children will take it in turns to play. Number 1 in the first group plays the tune, then number 1 in the second group and so on, continuing with number 2 in each group, then the 3s and 4s. As soon as a child has played she passes the beater on to the next person in the group. The whole class could join in the Batman yell and may also quietly whisper the:

> dinna dinna dinna dinna dinna dinna
> dinna dinna **BATMAN!**

Remember that while the children are learning this they should go more slowly than the pace at which they would normally sing it. To start off the practice ask the children to chant the theme together slowly. All the number 1s could play the tune through at the same time. If you do this, remember to insert one spoken version between each xylophone play so that there is time to pass on the beater to the number 2s. When everyone is confident with the theme ask them, in groups, to make up their own version of the tune – they can do this by arranging the notes in a different order, changing the rhythm, or both, to create a new tune.

Give the groups five minutes to practise their compositions, then ask each group to perform its new theme. Tell them that they should give the tune a name and, in order to do this, they will have to think what the tune is the theme

for. Ask them to consider whether it is a scary tune, a happy tune, an angry tune or a funny tune.

Tape the themes as the children play them. Many children will want to work individually on composing a theme, so this will be an ideal chance to use the chime bars or glockenspiels in a composing activity. Set up the instruments in a separate composing and listening corner. Leave the finished tape in the composing area and let the children listen and learn to play the new tunes, working by themselves or with a partner. They could also start to write down their tunes, perhaps putting them in a composition book which could be kept in the classroom music corner.

Suggestion(s) for extension

Children who complete this activity without difficulty could be encouraged to make up a two-part theme with two different tunes, both made up of the given notes. Ask them to arrange the two tunes in any order, playing one tune twice if they wish. They should also think up an exciting ending.

Alternatively, give them five notes and challenge them to make up a theme tune.

Suggestion(s) for support

If any children are struggling with the activity, play through the Batman theme with them again on *one* note, so that they are singing and playing the rhythm without having to change notes. Then play through the theme again, moving notes and singing the rhythm. When composing, ask them to arrange the notes in any order, changing their position if they wish.

Composing

Previous skills/knowledge needed

The children will need to have had some experience of using instruments and voices. The activities in the *Basic skills* chapter would provide useful background experience for children working at the easiest level. For those working at the higher level a number of activities would be helpful:

▲ 'Adventures in sound' (page 44) gives useful experience in exploring instrument sounds;

▲ 'Percussion band' (page 52) develops rhythmic skill and the ability to play together;

▲ 'Pass the beater' (page 49) looks at melodic shape;

▲ 'Sounds in a circle' (page 28) develops children's awareness of their voices as instruments;

▲ 'Patterns and rhythms' (page 62) explores ideas of structure.

Key background information

One of the best ways of extending children's musical skill and understanding is to give them plenty of opportunities to make use of what they know. The composition tasks in this activity draw on the children's developing skills and make use of the experience they will gain from other activities in this book.

This activity can be revisited again and again as the children's skills increase. To facilitate this the tasks have been written at three different levels. All the composition tasks are designed to be carried out, without teacher supervision, using materials available in the classroom music corner, and could easily be slotted in with other activities as part of an integrated day.

Assessment opportunities

This activity gives opportunities to assess children's ability to compose a simple tune and memorise and perform a rhythm. You should also be able to observe their control of an instrument, and note their awareness of structure in composing music, when they are asked to arrange two different tunes.

Opportunities for IT

The children could use a simple graphics package to create a score for their composition. If a drawing package is used it is helpful to turn on the background grid and 'snap to grid' option to help children line up their graphical symbols.

The children could also use a keyboard to create special sound effects to enhance the Batman effect.

Vocabulary

Composition, tune, rhythm, pattern, phrase.

Display ideas

In the music corner have a display of Batman cloaks as a background for 'zooming versions' of Batman themes. Use photographs of the children playing their tunes, possibly dressed in Batman costumes. Any notations the children have prepared, and tapes of the tunes, could be displayed there too.

Moving forward

Game 3 of 'Show time' (page 72) and 'Composition cards' (on this page) link well with the composing the children undertake in this activity. 'Talking about music' (page 88) extends the children's vocabulary for talking about music.

Composing

Preparation

Copy photocopiable pages 127, 128 and 129, cut them up, stick them on to card and cover them with clear adhesive film. Choose to make up one or more sets of the cards, according to the level at which children are working. Collect enough instruments for the composition tasks to be carried out (see 'Resources needed').

Resources needed

Set of composition cards (see 'Preparation'), about four tuned instruments (xylophone, chime bars, penny whistle, keyboard) and four untuned instruments (drums, tambourine, triangle, maracas), plain paper and writing materials (all these resources can be kept permanently in the classroom music corner), cassette player and blank tape (optional).

What to do

Introduce the composition cards to the whole class (you may choose to introduce just a few cards at a time) and ask the children for suggestions on how they might respond to the tasks. Make sure you read through all the cards with them, so they know what to expect when they come to use them independently. (Some children may need help in reading the cards again before they carry out the tasks, though the illustrations on the cards are designed to give as many clues as possible to the types of composition required.) Point out to the children that the list in the top left-hand corner of each card shows whether the task is to be carried out individually, in pairs or in groups. Remind the children that they must follow the instructions on the cards, and that they must keep their compositions in their heads (at least for long enough to be able to repeat them).

The results of the children's work with these cards can be used in a variety of ways.

▲ The children could perform their compositions to the rest of the class.

▲ The tasks could be used simply for exploration, without the need for a performance each time.

▲ The children could record their completed compositions and keep the tapes in the music corner for others to listen to. The composition cards can also be kept in the music corner.

▲ You could suggest that children use specific cards according to their skills and needs, or allow them to choose cards themselves and see how they get on.

Suggestion(s) for extension

As well as suggesting that children select cards at a higher level you can also encourage anyone who is coping easily with a composition task to add her own ideas to the composition. Children can also make up new composition cards for each other.

Suggestion(s) for support

Some children may need help at first to follow and interpret the instructions on the cards. It will help if you work alongside them, supporting them when they first use the cards, until they feel confident enough to use them independently.

Composing

Reference to photocopiable sheets

Photocopiable pages 127 to 129 provide a set of composition tasks at easy, medium and advanced levels.

Moving forward

Children can move from one level to another with the sets of cards, but their skills will also be developed by revisiting the same cards with the benefit of increased knowledge and skills. This activity links particularly well with 'Music corner cards' (page 103), which will help some children to grasp ideas of pattern and structure, as well as demonstrating some ways in which they might write out their compositions. 'Show time' (page 72) also links well with this activity as it uses a similar approach to composition. The children can further extend their compositional skills through 'Making waves' (page 74).

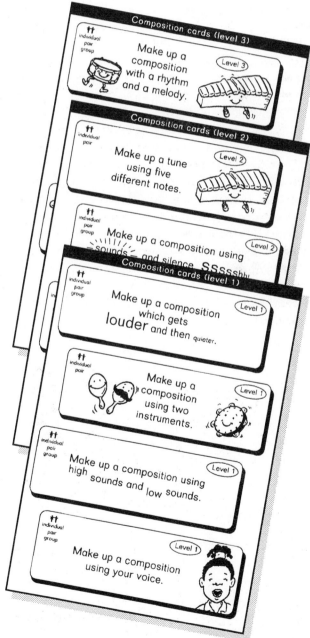

Assessment opportunities

As the children revisit this activity at different levels you will be able to monitor their ability to create increasingly complex compositions and to apply improving levels of skills and knowledge to their work.

Opportunities for IT

Set up a database of composition 'ingredients' on a computer (perhaps a list of words such as 'long sounds, short sounds, loud sounds, quiet sounds, rhythms, tunes, and so on) from which children can create their own 'composition recipes' for others to follow. The activity could be extended by allowing children to use a keyboard for some of their compositions or by using specific software such as Topologika's *Music Box*.

Display ideas

Extra copies of the composition cards and the children's own 'Composition recipes' (see 'Opportunities for IT') can be displayed in or near the classroom music corner, alongside children's written comments on their own and others' compositions. Where children have written down their compositions in some form, these can also be displayed.

Composing

In this activity percussion instruments which are usually found in the primary classroom have been used, but any means of making sounds could replace these well-known instruments. The aim of the activity is to encourage the children to use the sounds in increasingly complex ways so that by Game Three they will be able to create, write down and perform a rhythmic composition which involves two players playing at the same time.

Vocabulary
Perform, tambourine, chime bars, notes.

Preparation
Well before the game is played, photocopy the game board (photocopiable page 130), colour it in, back it with card, and cover it with clear adhesive film so that it can be used again and again. Take enough copies of the recording sheet (photocopiable page 131) for each player to have one. If you wish the players to work independently you could also photocopy a set of instructions for the games (photocopiable page 132).

To set up the game you will need to lay out the board with the instruments arranged round the side, so that the players can play them as the game is in progress. Each player needs access to a set of three chime bars, a tambourine, a drum, and a selection of other instruments. Obviously two players choosing, arranging and playing instruments will make less noise and also require fewer instruments than four, but when children have become familiar with Games One and Two they could ideally be played by four players, while Game Three would suit two or three pairs of players.

Resources needed
Game board (page 130), dice, a tambourine, three chime bars (C, D, and E) with a beater, small drum, one recording sheet for each player (page 131) pencils, one or more copies of the game rules (page 132).

What to do
Game One
The aim of this game is to collect enough instruments as you go round the board to play a composition using them all, when you reach the stage. The winner is the first person to do this and perform the composition.

To start: Throw the dice. The player with the highest number starts.

SHOW TIME

To introduce and develop the concept of composing, through different stages of difficulty.

† *In Games One and Two two, three or four individuals can play. In Game 3 teams of two play, although two or three teams could play at one time.*

🕓 *30 minutes for each game.*

♫ *Game One: easy*
Game Two: medium
Game Three: advanced.

Previous skills/knowledge needed
For Games One and Two 'Cut-and-paste composing' (page 60) would provide useful experience while 'Composition cards' (page 69) will help the players to work independently from the increasingly difficult instructions that accompany these games. 'Percussion band' (page 52) develops the players' ability to play together and record their compositions, both these skills are required for Game Three.

Key background information
Composing is really about choosing sounds and arranging them in a specific order for a particular reason. This reason will often be to communicate a mood, message, emotion or joke. The way the sounds are made can vary enormously, depending on the purpose of the composition.

Composing

The first player throws the dice and moves the correct number of squares round the board. If the player lands on a square which has a picture of an instrument, she picks up the instrument from the side of the board and plays it with a simple shake, bang, or rattle. The player has then 'collected' this instrument and is allowed to use it in the composition. To remind herself and other players of this, she records it on her recording sheet in any way she likes (perhaps a picture, a little symbol or the name of the instrument). The next player then throws the dice and the game continues. When the players have gone round the board they follow the path that leads into the stage. The first player to reach the stage performs her 'composition'. This will involve the child playing the instruments that she has collected and recorded as she has travelled round the board, in any order she likes. Each collected instrument may be played only once, but if she has landed on a tambourine square twice, then she must play a tambourine sound twice in the composition, if she landed on the drum only once then she may only play it once as part of the performance.

Other squares offer other options. If a player lands on a ? square she can make up any sound she likes, but it must be used in the same form in the performance. The picture of hands indicates that the child can make up any sound with hands. The practise squares aim to give the pupils opportunities to practise their composition so far. If they particularly want to change an instrument they may do this, but only if they land on the instrument swap square. When this happens they are allowed to swap any instrument on their recording sheet for any other one that is still beside the board.

The winner is the child who has collected most instruments and is able to use them all in the composition. It would not be appropriate to start judging the best composition. The aim of this game is to introduce the idea of choosing an order in which to put instruments, rather than discussing the finer points of creativity and what constitutes a masterpiece!

Game Two

Using the same basic method of playing the game, introduce the new condition that the children have to create a rhythm to play on each instrument. They should write this rhythm on the recording sheet, using any method that they choose. Dots and dashes for short and long notes can be helpful, though many children prefer the written form of Dum di, di, dum di di or dum di di di dum di dum or di di di di dum dum.

Once the rhythm has been recorded it should be played on every instrument, although the way in which it is played can be varied, fast, slow, loud or soft. On the board there is a shaded area of squares leading up to the stage. When a player lands on these squares he may use this turn to practise his rhythms and decide how to vary the playing of each one ready for performance when the stage is reached. The winner of the game is the player who reaches the stage first and is able to play the same rhythm on every instrument that he has collected.

Game Three (to be played in teams of two)

This variation builds on the skills learned in the previous games. As the children go round the board they make up a rhythm that they will both play together on the different instruments that they have collected. In addition, they must think of a way to record their rhythmic two-part composition so that the teacher and a chosen player can play it from their notation. This could act as a tie-breaker when the teams have a draw – at this point the notation of each piece would be handed over to an independent pair who would try to play the two pieces of notation. The more accessible notation would be the winner.

Suggestion(s) for extension

If children find all the games easy and are totally confident with the ideas, ask them to design their own music compositional board game.

Suggestion(s) for support

If children are finding the activity difficult, make small cut-outs of the instruments used on the board (cut them out from another photocopy and mount them). Use these cards instead of the recording sheet and, when it comes to the performance, support the child by laying out the cards and playing the instruments in order.

Assessment opportunities

This activity gives opportunities to assess whether a child understands the concept of composition as an activity in which sounds are arranged in a particular order. You should also be able to judge a child's ability to understand the concept of a picture or sign representing an instruction to play an instrument.

Display ideas

The board will be in constant use – it could be displayed alongside the instructions for use and recording sheets from the children's previous games.

Reference to photocopiable sheets

The board is on photocopiable page 130. This could be enlarged before being mounted, coloured and used. Photocopiable page 131 is the recording sheet with a simple layout of recording boxes laid out for each game and a box to record the rhythms for Game Two and the composition notation in Game Three. Photocopiable page 132 provides sets of instructions for the games.

Moving forward

Ask the children to make up their own games and try them out on each other. 'Mini orchestra' (page 55) develops the skill of playing together while 'Making waves' (on this page) uses notation and different combinations of instruments in more complex compositions.

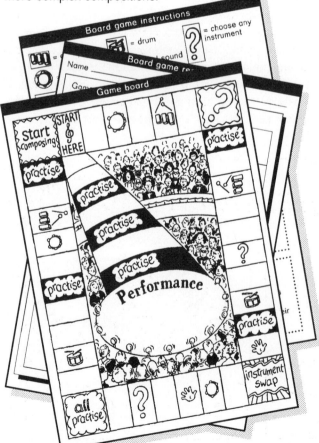

MAKING WAVES

To develop awareness of texture when composing to create a specific effect, from a stimulus of the child's own making.

†† *Small group to whole class.*

🕐 *Two 40-minute sessions.*

🎵 *Advanced.*

Previous skills/knowledge needed

'How does it sound?' (page 23) and 'Layers of sound' (page 25) would be good preparation for this activity. The use of timbre is explored further in 'Adventures in sound' (page 44) and in 'Sounds in a circle' (page 28). This activity makes use of graphic notation, introduced in the activity on page 100. The work covered in 'Talking about music' (page 88) will be useful when discussing the music.

Key background information

Music is often composed in response to, or to create a particular effect in, nature, emotion, or atmosphere. Using sound to 'paint a picture' is a popular concept and was used by many composers in the period known as the Romantic era of classical music. This term refers to music composed between about 1800 and 1900 and includes composers such as Beethoven, Brahms, Rachmaninov and Tchaikovsky.

The sea is a favourite subject for creating a 'sound picture'. It can be portrayed in a calm state as it is in the beginning of Debussy's piece *La Mer*, or as a storm, as in Wagner's overture to *The Flying Dutchman*. A term which can be used to describe this sort of descriptive classical music is 'tone poem'. Other examples are Debussy's piano piece *La Pluie* (Rain in the Garden), *Morning* from the *Peer Gynt Suite* by Grieg or Beethoven's *Pastoral Symphony, No 6*, in which an entire storm is portrayed.

Vocabulary

Texture, tone poem, describe, atmosphere.

Preparation

Collect together any stimulus you want to use to introduce the subject of the sea: perhaps a shell, a poem, a story, photographs or clothing. Decide which area of the subject you want to highlight. Prepare materials for painting and stimulus for the painting session. Have ready a recording of Debussy's *La Mer* (extract 9 on the tape) or any piece of music that gives the atmosphere of the sea. Provide a wide selection of instruments – both tuned and untuned percussion as well as any home-made instruments. Prepare one copy of the Listening comparison sheet (page 136) for each child.

Resources needed

Tape excerpt of *La Mer* by Debussy, painting materials, brushes, paper, selection of instruments, objects for stimulus, scissors, adhesive, one copy of photocopiable page 136 for each child.

What to do
Session One
Introduce the theme of the sea. Tell the children that you are going to paint a picture of the sea both in paint and in music. Ask them to think about what the sea is like, considering particularly the different parts of the sea, from the dark ocean floor with shells and coral to the lighter frothy water at the surface. Suggest that they close their eyes and 'see' their own picture of the sea inside their heads.

Encourage them then to think about the surface of their sea:
▲ Is it calm or stormy?
▲ Are the waves big or small?
▲ Is their picture in the middle of the sea, by some cliffs, next to a beach?
▲ Is there anything happening in the picture – are there any seagulls, people, boats, fish?
▲ What is the weather like?

Let the children start painting, either in small groups or as a whole class. Depending on the experience of the class you might prefer a small group of children to create the painting.

The finished picture might look rather like the one below. While the children are painting their pictures, ask them to think about how they will want to represent the different layers of their picture in music.
▲ Which things in the picture will you include in music?
▲ Which layer of the picture will need the loudest sound, the highest sound, a smooth sound, a jagged sound?

When they have finished the picture, ask them to decide on the instruments they will need for their composition. They may want more than one instrument for a particular part of the picture. As they decide, ask them to draw or make up a symbol to represent the instrument and cut it out with adult support as necessary.

Session Two
Look at the children's paintings and discuss how they have linked different instruments with different layers of the sea. Ask the children to place the symbols of the instruments that they cut out in the previous session in an appropriate place on the picture to show how each bit of picture will be represented. These can then either be stuck or attached in some other way in the correct place at the edge of the picture.

Ask the children to work in groups so that they can all play each other's compositions. Tell them to build up their composition layer by layer, starting with the instruments that represent the bottom of the sea, and working up from there. Ask the children to collect together the instruments required for composing one of the group's pictures and decide on an order in which to play the sounds. Encourage them to ask questions such as:
▲ How does the sound of the sea composition change as we add more layers to it?
▲ How are we going to know whether to be loud or soft in different layers?
▲ Are we making the sort of effect they had wanted to make?

There will be a lot of noise while all the children are experimenting, but you will find that the majority of children will be concentrating on the task.

Use a previously agreed sign to stop the composers and hear their work. Show all the group's pictures and, after the class has listened to a particular composition, ask the children to guess which of the pictures was being represented in music. When you have heard a number of the group's compositions, tell the children that they are going to listen

to someone else's sea music. Introduce the music and play a short section of Debussy's *La Mer* or the music that you have chosen.

Hand out copies of photocopiable page 136 and ask the children to compare Debussy's music with their own compositions. Ask questions such as:
▲ Were any of the same instruments chosen for both pieces?
▲ How did both pieces start?
▲ Was the music spiky, flowing, bouncy?

As they decide on answers to these questions they should fill them in on the photocopiable sheet. As the children finish this task, ask them whether they noticed any things that were the same, and compare the favourite parts of their two pieces.

This second session could be divided into two shorter sessions, but if you wish to do so it would be wise to tape the children's compositions when they play them and leave the Debussy comparison until the third session, or even let the children start their compositions but hear them at the beginning of the third session. Adapt the activity to suit yourself and your class!

Suggestion(s) for extension
In an activity like this differentiation is very much by outcome. Children who find this activity straightforward might be encouraged to compose mini theme tunes for different layers of the sea.

Suggestion(s) for support
If children find this activity difficult, suggest that they choose just three layers on the picture to represent in the composition.

Assessment opportunities
In this activity there are opportunities to assess children's awareness of texture in music, their skills in choosing instruments to represent certain things, and their ability to play and plan together.

Opportunities for IT
Some children might like to create their picture using an art package. This picture could then be imported into a multimedia authoring package and various sounds linked to the picture, then, by clicking on the bottom of the sea, the

children's composition for this part of the picture could be heard. The sounds could be recorded using a microphone attached to the computer.

Display ideas
Mount the descriptive words and symbols on the sea pictures to show which instruments were used to represent different parts of the picture.

Reference to photocopiable sheet
Photocopiable page 136 asks the children to write about the two pieces of music that they listened to so that a direct comparison can be made.

Moving forward
You could repeat the activity using a poem or piece of sculpture as the stimulus. This activity links well with 'Mini orchestra' (page 55) and 'Greasy chips' (page 41). 'Talking about music' (page 88) forms a natural progression from the children's discussion of their own work in this activity.

Listening

There are many different ways to listen to music – hearing, rather than listening to, background sound; half-listening to something as we continue with another job; intense and complete concentration.

The activities in this chapter acknowledge how much children have already learned from casual listening and build on this knowledge to develop more concentrated listening skills. The aim of these activities is not to make children *like* all the music they hear, but to enable them to listen to it, think about it, describe it and have an opinion about it.

Some of the music used may seem unfamiliar and inaccessible to the children at first, but as they learn to listen in different ways, it will become easier. The ideas given here can be used to listen to any number of different types of music: the pieces that are suggested here should simply be viewed as starting-points.

There are strong links between this and other chapters: the activities here make use of the playing and composing skills the children have developed elsewhere, while listening skills will be required in numerous other activities throughout this book.

INSTRUMENT ACTIONS

To develop more detailed listening skills and the ability to hear specific instrument tunes and rhythms.

†† *Whole class.*

🕐 *Two 20-minute sessions.*

♫ *Easy.*

Previous skills/knowledge needed

Any listening games or activities that encourage the children to listen to what they are hearing would support this activity. 'Starting and stopping' (page 14), 'Louder and softer' (page 20) and 'Layers of sound' (page 25) all encourage this skill.

Key background information

In music, one of the skills that often makes concentrated listening to music easier is being able to listen for a specific instrument and follow the pattern or tune of that instrument. Neither you nor the children need to know what the instrument is called – whether it is a tenor horn or a French horn is not important. The important thing is that both you and the children listen for the different sound made by the instrument and have a rough idea of what type of instrument it might be – brass, strings, drums, and so on. A range of posters, records and booklets give information about different instruments and local music shops often hire out instruments so may be willing to come and show what some of these

look like. The most famous pieces of music that demonstrate the instruments of the classical orchestra are Britten's *Young Person's Guide to the Orchestra* and Prokofiev's *Peter and the Wolf.* Many tapes, CDs and videos give information on instruments used in jazz or pop. Educational music publishers, record shops or libraries may have some suggestions. The extract provided on the cassette of *African Jungle* by the Jungle Town Stompers features a 1920s jazz band. The instruments featured are trumpet, trombone, 'reeds' (such as saxophones), piano, banjo and 'brass bass' (tuba).

Vocabulary

Different instrument names (depending on the music you are using). This example requires trumpet, saxophone, drum, cymbal.

Preparation

Choose a piece of music that has distinct instruments playing at different times to each other. The extract should not be any longer than three minutes, or the children will lose concentration. *African Jungle* by the Jungle Town Stompers is the jazz piece used in the explanation of the activity. This is extract 10 on the cassette.

It is not essential to listen to the music first, although it could increase your confidence. However, if you are not using the Jungle Town Stompers music you might prefer to listen to your chosen music so you can have formed some idea of what you want the children to be doing. Make copies of either Jazz band line-up or Instruments of the orchestra, photocopiable sheets 133 and 121 to suit the music you have chosen.

Resources needed

The selected music, cassette recorder or CD player and copies of the appropriate instrument identification sheet (photocopiable sheets 133 or 121) so the children can refer to them.

What to do
Session One

Seat the children so that they all can see each other and you as well. Tell them that you are going to play a short piece of music and that you want them to listen carefully to hear *which* instruments are playing and also *how* they are playing – loud, quiet, fast, slow.

If you are using the Stompers music, play the first 40 seconds of the music – a short section which is full of interest. The whole band plays the first chord and then the trumpet and saxophones have a short 'musical conversation' with

the tuba, both sides taking turns to speak and sometimes speaking at the same time. After a short while the whole band joins in but instruments such as the tuba and trombone continue to have short 'mini solos'.

After listening to this part of the extract show them the instrument identification sheet to help them realise what the instruments look like, then ask them:

▲ How many different sorts of instruments could you hear?
▲ How many people were playing?
▲ What sort of tunes or sounds were they playing?
▲ Were they long or short, spiky or smooth, loud or quiet?

Say that you are going to play it again and this time you want them to listen so that they can later pretend to be the instruments.

Play the first 40 seconds again, miming the trumpet players by holding your hands in front of your mouth.

Explain to the children that they are going to be like the band in the music – each child is going to pretend to play one instrument. For the activity a group of children will become one of the instruments played by a member of the jazz group in the extract on the tape. Divide the class into groups of trombonists, saxophonists, trumpeters, pianists, tuba and banjo players. Make sure you have a mixture of boys and girls in each group. Practise with each group, in turn, to show them how their instrument is played.

When the children first listen and mime the session will probably become a sea of flailing arms. Play the initial 40 seconds of the extract and then stop. Remind the children that they have to listen *really* carefully and stop *exactly* when

their instrument stops playing. Practise by playing the extract two or three times so the children can become familiar with their part.

Now hold another rehearsal and this time encourage the children to sit like performers before the music starts, and to lift up their 'instruments' when they are 'playing', especially the trumpets, so they will look like a jazz band.

Pause after this and talk about the music they are hearing.
▲ Is it happy or sad?
▲ Would it be good for going to sleep or dancing?

Remind the children that even though they are only pretending to play the instruments, the way they play and the care they take to start and stop at the right times is what makes the music really sound and look good.

If the children are fading at this point it would be a good place to stop the session and continue the activity in a second session.

Session Two

After the first 40 seconds come a series of solos. The trumpet takes the lead while the rest of the band plays an accompaniment. Within this accompaniment, however, there are times when individual instruments have short passages of solo playing. The trombone, tuba then piano and banjo, all have short periods where a single instrument can be heard clearly.

This type of music lends itself to the traditional jazz band practice of soloists, or whole sections of the band, standing up to play the solos, even if this involved only a few notes.

As the music becomes more familiar to both you and the children the possibilities of what you can do in the mime become greater. You could introduce the notion of a conductor who points at the trumpeters to stand up and sit down at the correct time. In some jazz bands one section sits down as another section stands up and, with practice, the children would enjoy doing this.

Bear in mind that the basis of all the mime and staging is to enhance their listening so all movements should be related to what is happening in the music.

As a final performance, play the whole thing through complete with a flourish at the end and a bow from the

children. This final performance would provide an excellent photo opportunity to show what they had been doing.

Suggestion(s) for extension

If the children are not stretched by the activity give them a similar piece of music and ask them to work out a mime for themselves. Remind them that they should be showing the instruments that are played in the music. If you give them a free choice of music it is likely that you will get a copy of a pop video. This can be an extremely good and creative activity for dance or drama but is very different from asking them to listen and mime the actual instruments as they play. Beware of merely repeating what they are already doing rather than challenging their listening skills.

Suggestion(s) for support

If the children are finding the activity hard ask them to be one of the instruments that is most obvious in its sound. In the case of the Jungle Town Stompers the trumpet would be the most obvious instrument.

Assessment opportunities

This activity provides the opportunity to assess whether the children can listen carefully and recognise when particular instruments are playing, also whether they are aware of the skills involved in staging a good performance.

Opportunities for IT

The children could use a CD-ROM such as Microsoft's *Musical Instruments* to explore sounds made by other instruments.

Display ideas

Use photographs of the children 'performing' as a basis for an interactive display. Provide a cassette recorder, with the cassette of the music used, beside the display, and challenge people to guess which part of the music is represented by the photographs.

Reference to photocopiable sheets

Photocopiable page 133 provides a picture of a typical 1920s jazz band line-up to help children with instrument identification. Photocopiable page 121 offers an orchestral version of the same thing.

Moving forward

'Going round in circles' (page 86) asks the children to respond to music with actions, while 'Join the band' (page 84) asks the children to play along, after listening to specific rhythms in the music. This activity also links well with 'Instrument pictures' (page 96).

HEADS AND TAILS

To develop listening skills which recognise differences in melody, such as verse and chorus.

†† *Whole class.*

⏱ *15 minutes.*

♫ *Easy.*

Previous skills/knowledge needed

Any games that develop the idea of listening intently to a tune such as 'Patterns and rhythms' (page 62) would be helpful for this. Any other singing activity would also be good preparation.

Key background information.

The skill of listening entails many different things. In the context of music education, being able to distinguish different tunes, and different parts of a tune, is an important part of being able to play tunes and listen and talk about music of any sort. Listening to a tune as you sing it is one of the basic skills of performing. In this activity the form of verse and chorus is used as the listening point using the well-known sea shanty 'What shall we do with the drunken sailor?'

Verse and chorus refer to the layout of the words. The recurring refrain:

> Hurray and up she rises
> Hurray and up she rises
> Hurray and up she rises
> Early in the morning

is the chorus. The changing words in between form the verses.

Verse 1: What shall we do with the drunken sailor
(three times)
Verse 2: Put him in the long boat until he's sober
(three times)
Verse 3: Put him in the scuppers with the hose pipe on him (three times)

All forms of music use the verse and chorus structure, though many songs have no chorus at all. Folk tunes often have a chorus, as do many classical songs, African chants and pop songs. When choosing the music you want to work with don't rule out the possibility of using the current Number One if it is a song with a chorus.

Vocabulary
Verse, chorus, repeated, same, different.

Preparation
Choose a song with a verse and chorus. Learn it well so that you can teach it to the children if they don't already know it. It is often better to start with a song the children are familiar with. This explanation uses 'What shall we do with the drunken sailor?'

Resources needed
A song with a verse and chorus, a coin.

What to do
Explain to the children that you are about to have a singing session and that you want them to listen particularly carefully to the song, and how the tune and words fit, because you are going to ask them some questions about it at the end. Sing the song that you have chosen and, at the end, ask them which part of the song is repeated. If they do not know sing it again with them, asking them to listen for the one set of words that comes back after the changed words. In many tunes, including 'What shall we do with the drunken sailor', parts of the tune are repeated in each verse, but the important difference is that the words change with each verse while the chorus words and tune remain the same.

Once they have identified the repeated chorus, split the class into two. Ask one half to sing only the verse and the other half only the chorus. Sing the song again and try to observe whether the children are aware in advance of when they should sing or whether they are merely following your directions.

Introduce the words 'verse' and 'chorus' as new music vocabulary. Reinforce the new words through simple games of how quickly the correct group can all put their hands up when you say chorus, (or verse) or how quickly they can sing the first word of their section when you say chorus (or verse). Once you think that most of the class understand the different parts of the song, start the Heads and Tails game.

Decide whether the verse is going to be heads or tails and make it clear to the class which part of the song goes with which call of the coin. Ask a child to toss the coin and call – the appropriate side then has to start singing their part of the song immediately, be it verse or chorus. As soon as the class have got the hang of the game, spin the coin three times in a row to see how the song should be sung next. You may get a combination of chorus, chorus, verse, or you may get three verses with no chorus at all. Whatever comes up on the coin must be followed!

After you have sung two combinations of the reworked song ask the children what it sounds like when you have no chorus or nothing but chorus.

▲ Does it sound more interesting or less interesting?

▲ Do they like singing it more or less?

As a grand finale spin the coin five times and have the whole class sing whatever order of verse and chorus is dictated by it.

Suggestion(s) for extension

Any children who find the activity easy could be asked to listen to what is being sung without being told the coin combination. Then challenge them to write down the order of the combination that they are hearing. They could also think of their own song with verse and chorus and play the same game in a small group.

Suggestion(s) for support

If the children are finding the activity too difficult then go back to using the two halves of the class to sing verse and chorus at your direction. One of the children might give the commands 'verse' and 'chorus'.

Assessment opportunities

This activity provides an opportunity to check that the children can distinguish between verse and chorus.

Display ideas

The structure of verse and chorus could be displayed visually through artwork which portrays the different parts of the song with a repeated design used for the chorus.

Moving forward

Repeat this exercise using different songs. 'Morning song' (page 35) and 'Join the band' (page 84) invite the children to join in with the choruses of the songs.

🎧 JOIN THE BAND

To help children feel the rhythm of a piece of music.
†† *Whole class.*
🕐 *10–20 minutes (depending on whether you introduce instruments).*
🎵 *Medium.*

Previous skills/knowledge needed

The children need to understand the idea of keeping a steady beat, though they may not yet be very good at it. 'Keeping the beat' (page 18) provides an excellent introduction to this activity and you might like to consider running the two together into a single session. If the children have also tried 'Heads and tails' (page 81), they will be more aware of the verse – chorus structure of the song used here. 'Instrument actions' (page 78) also reinforces skills the children will need for this activity.

Key background information

Young children find it surprisingly difficult to clap or play in time with a piece of music. They will often clap along with great enthusiasm, but without actually feeling the rhythm of the music. This activity develops both children's listening skills, and their rhythmic awareness, by encouraging them to listen carefully and feel the beat before they join in with sounds of their own. The activity invites the children to move, clap, then play in time with the music, although it may be easier not to introduce instruments until you have carried out this activity a number of times.

You can use any piece of rhythmic music for this: a song with a chorus that also has a strong rhythmic feel to it would be particularly suitable. This activity uses a Hoagy Carmichael song called *The Old Music Master*, (excerpt 11 on the cassette). It tells the story of a little boy who steps back in history from his own time (the 1930s – the heyday of jazz) to advise the Old Masters that they should make their music swing (incorporating an outrageous rhyme between 'spinet' and 'infinite' along the way!). The reference to a 'little coloured boy' in the lyrics is characteristic of songs of this era. The language of the song will seem out of date today, with its overtones of racial discrimination, but will provide a good basis for discussion.

Vocabulary

Beat, rhythm, movement, verse, chorus.

Preparation

Listen to the song on the tape and practise clapping or playing along with the chorus yourself. If you are going to use instruments (see 'Key background information' above), check you have enough for the whole class.

Resources needed

Cassette player, the recording of *The Old Music Master* on the cassette which accompanies this book (or a recorded song or tune of your own choice), enough untuned percussion instruments for the whole class (if appropriate).

What to do

Tell the children that you are going to play them a song which is all about music. The first time just play the song through, letting them listen and enjoy it. They will probably sit fairly still during the verses, which are quite slow, but automatically jiggle about during the choruses, which are much more lively.

Play the song again, but this time move in time to the music *only during the choruses*, as this makes the structure of the song clear. The children can sit or stand to join in with the movement.

The next time through ask them to clap, and move, during the choruses. Do this yourself, exaggerating your movements and clapping so they can see how you keep in time with the music: this works best if you all stand up and dance! If you find this just degenerates into random clapping without any feeling for the rhythm, go back to just moving and encourage the children to move *together*, as if they were all parts of one giant machine. When they are doing this confidently, bring the clapping back in, keeping it carefully in time with the movements. You can either finish the session here or introduce instruments at this point.

If you decide to use instruments, stop the tape, sit the children down again and give out an instrument to each child. Let them all play together for a minute or so to get the feel of their instruments: you can practise stopping and starting signals here and even volume control if you like. See 'Starting and stopping' (page 14) and 'Louder and softer' (page 20) for ideas.

Now ask the children to put their instruments down but be ready to play them at your signal. Play the song again, keeping still during the verses and playing *in time with the music* during the choruses.

Repeat this as many times as you like (possibly over several days or even several weeks) and finish with a grand performance in which everyone stands still in the verses, and moves, claps or plays in the choruses according to your choice. You can even add in some rhythmic dance steps devised by yourself or the children once they are confident with moving and playing.

Suggestion(s) for extension
Children who are keeping the beat well can be asked to make up a more complex rhythm for the choruses. Remind them that they still need to keep in time with the music. They might devise a rhythm something like this:

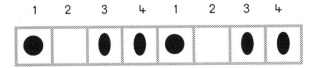

Suggestion(s) for support
Some children will continue to find it hard to keep in time with the music. The very best way to support these children is to give them plenty of opportunities to practise. The more times you carry out this activity, or other similar work, the better they will get.

Assessment opportunities
During this activity, monitor the children's ability to feel the rhythm of a piece of music, to move in time with it, to keep a steady beat using hands and instruments and to follow signals from a conductor.

Display ideas
Photographs of the children moving, clapping and playing will remind them of what it feels like to keep in time with the music. You could also display the words of the chorus with the strong beats underlined, or marked with hand claps or other symbols: for example;

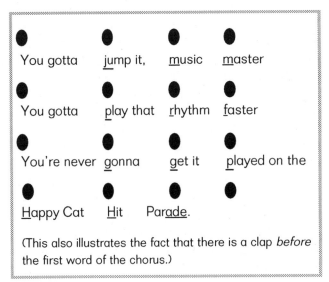

●	●	●	●
You gotta	<u>jump</u> it,	<u>music</u>	<u>master</u>
You gotta	<u>play</u> that	<u>rhythm</u>	<u>faster</u>
You're never	<u>gonna</u>	<u>get</u> it	<u>played</u> on the
<u>Happy</u> Cat	<u>Hit</u>	Pa<u>rade</u>.	

(This also illustrates the fact that there is a clap *before* the first word of the chorus.)

Opportunities for IT
The children could use a word processor to write out the words of the chorus, with the strong beats highlighted by use of underlining, bold, colour or a larger font size.

Moving forward
This activity can be repeated any number of times, using any music in which the rhythm can be heard clearly. (This might include slow music, such as a slow waltz, as well as faster pieces.) The more experience the children have of keeping in time, the more their skills will develop. This aspect of the activity links particularly well with 'Patterns and rhythms' (page 62) and 'Percussion band' (page 52), while the children's listening skills can be developed further through 'Talking about music' (page 88).

GOING ROUND IN CIRCLES

To develop awareness of structure in music.
†† *Whole class.*
⏰ *20 minutes.*
♫ *Medium.*

Previous skills/knowledge needed
This activity requires skill in listening to the different changes that occur within music. 'Heads and tails' (page 81) introduces the idea of listening and responding to different tunes within singing. 'Instrument actions' (page 78) uses actions to respond to the different instruments heard within music.

Key background information
All music, even the most avant-garde, has a formal organisation of some sort. Many songs and pieces of instrumental music have two parts – one main tune, followed by another main tune which is similar but different in pitch and melody to the first. These tunes are often referred to as tune A and tune B. The way in which tunes A and B are arranged is the *structure* of the music.

Obviously there may be more than two tunes, but these additions are often based on, or developed from, tunes A and B. Occasionally a tune C is introduced to add to the interest of the piece. In this activity the idea of the structure is not spoken about in these terms. The most important thing is that the children develop an awareness that the tune changes, and that the tune occurs again and again. They should end up going round in circles just like the tune!

Vocabulary
Repeat, tune, melody.

Preparation
Listen to the tune of 'Where I laid on Greenland's coast' from the *Beggar's Opera*, extract 12 on the cassette (the children may know this as *Tom, Tom the piper's son*). Check that you can hear the two major tunes that occur. The first tune, tune A, is repeated before tune B starts at a much higher pitch, but using the same jumpy rhythm.

Resources needed
Recording of 'Where I laid on Greenland's coast' from the *Beggar's Opera*, cassette recorder.

What to do
Seat the children in a circle. If you have already carried out the 'Heads and tails' activity (page 81), remind the children of what they did, and of how the two groups sang the different parts of the song. Explain that they are going to be doing a similar sort of thing in this activity. Ask them to listen carefully to the music that you are going to play. Point out that you

are only going to play it for a short time so they must listen as hard as they can to hear things in the music which will tell them what to do next in the activity. Play the music once and then, without passing comment, other than positive remarks about how well individuals listened, play it again.

After the second playing ask the children if they could hear where the tune changes in the middle of the music. They will probably say 'yes' whether they can or not, but at this stage this does not matter. Say that you are going to play the music again and, this time, ask them to put up their hands when the music changes.

This part of the activity provides an excellent informal opportunity for assessing which children understand what you mean and, more importantly, the nature of the understanding of the rest of the class. Often the language that teachers use in music lessons can mislead children. A child's hand may well go up in the middle of the first tune because he feels the music changes at that point and, in fact, it does, even though it is not officially the end of tune A. Bear in mind that the process is more important than the correct answer, so if the child is really listening attentively accept what he says, while making it clear that for this session the repeat of the tune occurs when the whole of tune A is finished.

After this third hearing choose one of the children who raised a hand at the end of the first tune or who you feel is understanding the activity. Tell him that he is person A and this time when the music is played he should get up and run round the outside of the circle every time he hears the first tune (tune A is repeated so the child will have to run around twice each time the music is played). Ask another child to be person B and tell her that she will run round the circle every time the second tune is played (the child will also have to run round twice). Play the music again and let the children run. The first time they do this things will probably be rather chaotic, so repeat the activity using the same children.

Then ask the rest of the class if any of them think they can run at the correct time without help. Let the volunteers have a go, and continue the activity like this. The children will gradually get used to hearing the place where the different runners should start. As the children become more confident, let them run in groups of three or four. This will also support those who are not so confident.

As a grand finale, turn the volume of the music up as high as other teaching groups will permit and have everyone running as either an A or B person and then sitting totally silently back in their places as the music stops.

Suggestion(s) for extension
Children who find the activity easy could be asked to think of a favourite song or tune and work out where in the music they would have different people running around. They might be able to bring in their music and, with your help, run the activity again using the new music.

Suggestion(s) for support
If you notice children who are finding the activity difficult, do not ask them to run until they have heard the music four or five times. Let them run in partnership with a more confident person.

Assessment opportunities

This activity provides opportunities to assess whether the children have understood this basic introduction to the structure used in music and their ability to recognise changes of tune in music.

Opportunities for IT

The words of the chorus could be printed out as above using a computer.

Display ideas

Take photographs of the children running and provide a simple written explanation of what is going on. If possible, provide a cassette recorder with the cassette so that viewers of the display can listen to the music for themselves.

Moving forward

This activity can be repeated a number of times, using any music in which the rhythm can be heard clearly (try using slow music, such as a slow waltz, as well as faster pieces). The more experience the children have of keeping in time, the more their skills will develop. As they become more aware they can move on to 'Talking about music' (on this page). This activity links particularly well with 'Patterns and rhythms' (page 62) and 'Percussion band' (page 52).

TALKING ABOUT MUSIC

To develop children's ability to use vocabulary and express opinions about the music they are listening to.

♯♯ *Whole class or small groups of four or five.*

🕐 *Two 20-minutes sessions.*

♫ *Advanced.*

Previous skills/knowledge needed

Any language work that has involved description of mood, emotion or talking about artwork will support this activity. Many of the activities in the Basic skills chapter would reinforce the work. In addition, any activity that has involved listening carefully to music, such as 'Join the band' (page 84) or 'Going round in circles' (page 86) would all support this activity well.

Key background information

One of the hardest things that children are asked to do when listening to music is to talk about what they have heard. Music by its very nature is unrelated to speech.

There are two main problems that are encountered when anyone is asked to talk about music; first the difficulty of identifying the part of the music they are talking about and, second, having the vocabulary to express what they want to say. The range of words that could be used to describe sounds in music are enormous – even wider than children would be expected to use in their stories or poetry at this age.

This activity is split into two sessions, although the first session could be tried several times before the second session is introduced. In Session One descriptive words are brainstormed, then recorded by writing them on to an Opinion or Comparison sheet. In Session Two these words are used to support the children in comparing pieces of music, giving their opinion, or both. Choose a means of recording thoughts from the range of photocopiable sheets.

Vocabulary

Description, opinion, as many descriptive words as you and the children can think of.

Preparation

For Session One you will need to choose a piece of music to listen to. Any music on the tape that accompanies the book would be suitable or you can choose your own. Make an A3 list of descriptive words written in an expressive form. Photocopiable page 134 has some examples which could be enlarged and coloured in. If you cut these out and cover them with clear adhesive film they will last for many sessions and can become a school music resource. You will also need to make one copy of the Listening report sheet (page 154) for each child.

For Session Two you will need to choose two contrasting pieces of music, possibly *Imaginary Landscape No2 (1942)* by John Cage and *La Mer* by Debussy, which are both on the tape that accompanies the book. Choose either the Listening comparison sheet (page 136) which accompanies the 'Making waves' activity (page 74) or the Listening opinion sheet (page 135), and make one copy for each child. If the children have not tried the activity before use the opinion sheet.

Resources needed

Paper, pencils and colouring materials, cassette recorder.
Session One: Two sheets of A3 paper, one Listening report sheet (page 154) per child, your chosen music.
Session Two: A3 sheet of descriptive words, felt-tipped pen, one Listening opinion or Listening comparison sheet (pages 135 and 136) per child, your chosen music (this could be the same piece as in Session One).

What to do
Session One

Show the children your A3 list. Go through all the words and check that the children can read them, and know what they mean. Explain to the children that they are going to listen to a piece of music, and that you want them to choose some of the words which match the music. More importantly, however, you want them to think of their own words to describe the music so that these can be added to the list.

Play the music. After the first playing ask all the children to tell you one word that says what the music is like. These could either be words already on the A3 sheet or new words. Expect suggestions such as happy, sad, fast or slow but encourage the class to use wider-ranging words such as bubbly, spiky, wobbly or sharp. As each word is suggested, ask the child to write it on a piece of A4 paper, making it into a particular shape as the other words are. Alternatively, write the word yourself then ask the child to copy it, in big writing,

to go on to the sheet. As each new word is completed, cut it out and place it on the A3 sheet, attaching it with Blu-Tack or small loops of masking tape. If the sheet becomes too full ask the children to start new smaller sheets of music words.

Now play the music again and ask the children to start to think of three words to describe it, either from the list on the A3 sheet or using words that they have thought up for themselves.

Give out a Listening report sheet (page 154) to each child and ask them to fill in the first three spaces (either with the help of an adult scribe or by writing independently). Tell them you are going to play the music one more time and that this time you want them to decide on the three descriptive words and fill these in on their listening report. They should also draw in the face that represents their opinion of the music. Emphasise that the descriptive words don't need to match their opinion of the music. They might use the words 'slow, scary and spiky' but still have the 'like it' smiling face, or have the words 'happy, light and tuneful' with the 'don't like it' frowning face.

To finish the session ask the children to compare their sheet with their neighbour's. Ask them questions such as:

▲ Did you choose the same words?

▲ Were there any unexpected words?

▲ Did your neighbour have the same opinion as you?

Emphasise here also that it is fine for different children to have different opinions about the music. Use the children's work to show examples of interesting descriptive words and add any new words to the A3 sheet. Pin up the listening reports so that the children can all look at each other's work.

Session Two

Remind the children briefly of the work covered in the previous session if this is appropriate, or show them the A3 word sheet. Play the piece of music that you are using for the session. (This could be the same piece as in the last session, since familiarity will help the children to see themselves as experts and should give them confidence to say more about the music, but feel free to choose a completely new piece of music.) After hearing the music, discuss with the children which of the words on the A3 word sheet they would use to describe this piece of music. If they appear quite confident you could ask them to discuss, in groups of four, for a couple of minutes, then report back using one member of the group as spokesperson.

Tell the children that you now want them to listen to the music in more detail, so that they can give a more detailed opinion. Explain that you are going to play the extract of music three more times. The first time you particularly want them to listen to the way it begins:

▲ Is it fast or slow?

▲ Is it loud or soft?

▲ What sort of sounds are made – tinkly, like a bell: plip, plop like rain or a crisp clip clop like horses' hooves? (These are a few ways of describing timbre.)

▲ Are there a few instruments or lots of instruments?

▲ Is the music spiky or smooth, rich or plain?

After this first time of playing discuss with the class what they thought of the beginning of the music and add to the A3 wordsheet any new words or phrases that might be useful. If space is short start a new sheet. If the class appears confident with this give out the Listening opinion sheets (page 135) or Listening comparison sheets (page 136) and ask the children to fill in the first opinion balloon (the beginning). Otherwise, fill in one Listening opinion sheet for the class. The listening, opinion-making and talking about the music is what is really important – the writing down is merely a convenient and enjoyable form of recording. Alternatively, try recording the children's views or listen to what they have to say.

Repeat the process for listening to the end of the extract, but this time add questions such as:

▲ Was the beginning using the same sounds and instruments as the end?

▲ Was the feeling the same at the end as at the beginning?

During the third and final playing ask the children to think for themselves what their favourite part of the music was (perhaps a particular instrument sound or a repeated tune) and for their opinion of the piece overall. This could also be the time to ask what the piece made them think of, perhaps of a colour, or a mood.

When the sheet or sheets are completed, play the music one more time for the children to listen to as experts who know their material. If they wish to join in by singing or tapping a rhythm let them do so provided, of course, that this doesn't prevent others from listening.

Suggestion(s) for extension

Children might be able to work through the process themselves with new pieces of music in the class music corner. The music used could be their choice from home or school or something that you give to them. As they listen to different pieces they could add to the class music listening book (see 'Display ideas', below).

Suggestion(s) for support

Children having difficulty could concentrate on using a few highly colourful words such as prickly or smooth which can be easily understood and represented. On the opinion and comparison sheets decide on a few simple sentences, such as:

▲ I thought the music had good tunes;

▲ I liked the sound of...;

▲ I found the music hard/easy to listen to.

Ask the children to write these words for you or colour in words you have written and place them on the sheet where they feel they should go. Many children will prefer to have the opportunity to record their opinions on a cassette recorder.

Assessment opportunities

This activity provides an opportunity to assess children's ability to talk about music and express opinions about what they hear.

Display ideas

The A3 music wordsheets will make an excellent colourful display. In addition, make a class book called 'Music Reports and Opinions', which can be the file for the class, or individuals' completed sheets.

Opportunities for IT

The children could use a word processor to design their own listening report, opinion or comparison sheets. They could also use a word processor or drawing package to make labels for a class display about a particular piece of music, presenting the words they have chosen to describe the music in different fonts, sizes or colours to enhance the range of expression in the selected words.

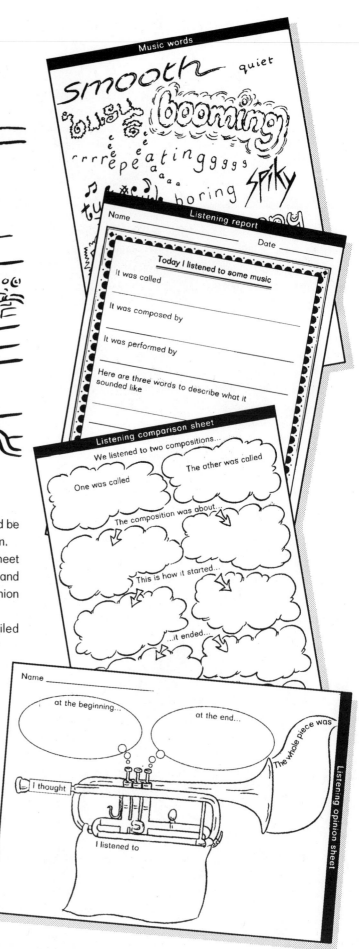

Reference to photocopiable sheets

'Music words' (page 134) gives a list of words that could be used to describe music, written out in a descriptive form.

Listening report sheet (page 154) is a simple factual sheet asking for details of the music, composer and performer and three descriptive words, as well as the child's overall opinion in the form of an expressive face.

Listening opinion (page 135) requires more detailed descriptions which are written into thought balloons under the headings of beginning, end and the whole piece.

Listening comparison sheet (page 136) asks for a mixture of factual details, descriptions and opinions about the music.

All these photocopiable sheets would be appropriate for use with the children's own compositions or with any other type of music.

Moving forward

Repeat the activity as many times as you wish using two different pieces of music and extending the vocabulary used each time. Refer back to words that have been used for previous pieces. This activity links particularly well with 'Making waves' (page 74) and 'Mini orchestra' (page 55) in which the children are invited to discuss and evaluate their own compositions.

Notation

The aim of this chapter is to remove one of the major barriers to both adults and children seeing themselves as musical. Traditionally, music education was thought of as learning formal notation: the dots and stalks found in a book of piano music. Thankfully, the National Curriculum has confirmed that this is not what music education is about. Formal notation is touched on here, but most of the activities in the chapter use informal notation – the use of simple symbols to represent sounds in a flexible way. Notation can be used in two ways: to record what has already been composed and as a means of composition in itself. In this chapter, both uses are introduced and explored.

Young children find the concept of notation quite difficult, as it involves connecting a sound system with a system of symbols. For this reason most of these activities are demanding, but this does not mean that either the children or the teacher need have any specialised musical knowledge. As in all the other chapters, the activities here reinforce skills and understanding developed elsewhere, and links with other activities are clearly shown.

RAINDROPS

To introduce children to the principle of pitch notation.

†† *Whole class.*

🕐 *15 minutes.*

♫ *Easy.*

Previous skills/knowledge needed

Children need to have an awareness of high and low pitch for this activity. This can be developed through 'High and low' (page 15).

Key background information

This activity takes one of the basic principles of formal notation – that the notes on a stave go up and down like the notes in the music – and explores it without the constraints of the stave itself. It is not necessary to know the names of notes in order to grasp this principle or to carry out this activity: you just need to look at their relationship to each other.

Vocabulary

Note, high, low, pitch.

Preparation

Make four photocopies of page 137 and stick them together end-to-end, to form one long strip. (Turn the second and fourth sheet upside down, to vary the pattern.)

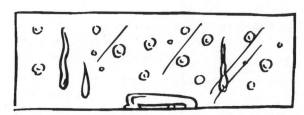

Resources needed

Four copies of photocopiable sheet 137.

What to do

Start the session by asking the children to sing some very high notes, then some very low notes, then some notes in between. You might like to consolidate the concept of high and low using hand gestures (see 'Pitch dance', page 34). Now hold up the photocopied sheet so that the length hangs down and all the children can see it (it doesn't matter which end you hold). Point out the shapes on the page and suggest they look like raindrops on a window pane.

Tell the children that you want them to sing high notes when you point to the 'raindrops' at the top of the sheet, low notes at the bottom and 'in-between' notes in the middle.

Point to the 'raindrops' at random, singing high, low or medium notes as appropriate while you point. If the children get the idea quickly, stop singing yourself and let them continue without you.

Now turn the sheet sideways, and hold it stretched out (or ask two children to take an end each). Again, it doesn't matter which way up it is. Tell the children that they are going to do the same as before, but point out that this time the high notes and the low notes are much closer together. You can demonstrate this by singing notes for the first few blobs before you ask them to join in. Work all the way from one end of the sheet to the other, singing notes at appropriate pitches as the children follow your finger. (These do *not* represent an exact pitch, as they are not on the lines of a stave: it is the relationship of each note to the next that is important.)

Conclude the session by experimenting with different ways of reading the score:

▲ split it into sections and assign different sections to different groups;

of pitch notation. (Some children find reading single blobs like this much easier than reading words on a page so the activity may even help to develop their reading confidence in general.)

Opportunities for IT

The children could use a painting or drawing package to undertake this work, creating their own symbols or using symbols taken from a clip art collection. Long scores will need to be printed out on separate pages and then joined together so children will need to know how to move symbols up and down the paper to show the variations in pitch.

Some 'Banner' type programs, which are used for making long titles, could also be used to create very long scores. Alternatively, you could use pictures in a word processor printed out on a printer with continuous paper feed, but in this case the symbols would have to be moved across the page so that, when the paper is printed and rotated by 90 degrees, the symbols are seen to move up and down the paper. To get around this problem, sheets could also be printed on separate pages and then joined together.

Display ideas

If the children have made their own graphic scores these can be displayed with the photocopiable sheets (mounted both vertically and horizontally) to demonstrate pitch differences. The ends of the sheets can also be joined together to form circular scores which can then be read continuously, or can be displayed on a turntable.

▲ ask some children to sing the high notes, some to sing the middle and some the low ones;
▲ ask each child to choose a particular type of note and sing it whenever the conductor points to it.

When you have run through this activity a number of times, invite the children to take turns as conductors, and to experiment with different ways of reading the score themselves.

Suggestion(s) for extension

Children who have coped well with this activity can make their own graphic scores, representing both high and low notes, and experiment with ways of singing or playing from them.

Suggestion(s) for support

Children who are having difficulty with this will derive particular benefit from being the conductor: this will enable them to hear the result when they point to high or low notes, as well as giving them a sense of control which will help to build their confidence.

Assessment opportunities

This activity will enable you to gauge the children's ability to respond to visual symbols and their awareness of the principles

Reference to photocopiable sheet

Photocopiable page 137 can be used both for this activity and for display purposes. It shows a random selection of blobs (notes) which represent both high and low sounds. These are distributed in such a way that when the page is turned sideways, there is still a difference in their height on the page.

Moving forward

This activity leads directly into 'Music corner cards' (page 103) and 'Reading a song' (page 105). Both these activities continue to explore the principle of notation, with 'Reading a song' (page 105) demonstrating how the principle applies to formal notation. This activity also links particularly well with 'Pitch dance' (page 34).

Raindrops notation

INSTRUMENT PICTURES

To introduce children to the principle of playing from visual symbols.

†† *Whole class.*

🕐 *15 minutes.*

♫ *Easy*

Previous skills/knowledge needed

The children need to recognise pictures of instruments for this activity. 'Cut-and-paste composing' (page 60) will help them to do this. They also need to be able to follow a conductor's signals. 'Starting and stopping' (page 14) and 'Louder and softer' (page 20) are particularly useful for this, and there are further hints on the Conducting sheet (page 114).

Key background information

This activity introduces the simplest possible use of symbols to represent sound: pictures of the instruments themselves. The intention here is to get the children used to responding to a visual stimulus: the *type* of sound they make on each instrument is of secondary importance. Four instrument pictures have been chosen to represent the sounds for this activity: a drum, a triangle, a tambourine and a cymbal. You may wish

to make additional instrument pictures to represent a wider range (see 'Preparation'). Once the children are familiar with the use of these cards, they can be displayed in the classroom music corner and used independently by the children.

Vocabulary

Drum, triangle, tambourine, cymbal, instrument.

Preparation

Copy photocopiable page 138 (enlarging it if you wish), cut it up and stick each instrument picture on to card. (Alternatively, draw each instrument picture on to card.) The pictures could be coloured in to make them more attractive. If you want to use a wider range of instruments than the four shown on the photocopiable sheet, you will need to make additional instrument cards to represent them.

Have a collection of drums, triangles, tambourines and cymbals (and other instruments if you are using them) ready for the class to play.

Resources needed

One set of instrument cards (see 'Preparation') and one instrument (of the type represented on the cards) for each child.

What to do

Before you give out any instruments, show the instrument cards to the children and ask them to identify the pictures. Now give out the instruments in groups (all the drums together, all the triangles together, and so on) but ask the children not to play them until you tell them to do so. Once they have all got instruments, give the children an opportunity to play them freely together for a minute or two to prevent them from becoming frustrated waiting for their turn later in the activity. Stop them with a signal (see 'Starting and stopping' (on page 14) or the Conducting sheet (page 114), and tell them that you are now going to use the instrument cards as signals for each group of instruments to play.

Demonstrate this with one group at a time. It doesn't matter what the children play on their instruments, as long as the drums play when you hold up the drum picture, and so on.

As the children get used to responding to the instrument cards, you can increase the speed with which you change from card to card – you can even hold up two cards at a time. It is also a good idea to swap the instruments around, so that each child gets a chance to play more than one. Conclude the activity by inviting some of the children to take turns as conductors.

Suggestion(s) for extension

Children who follow the cards easily can use them in the music corner to devise simple sequences of sounds which can then be played by small groups. (This is the same principle as is used in 'Cut-and-paste composing', page 60.) It will help to have a stand to place the cards on, so the sequence can be seen clearly.

Suggestion(s) for support

Some children will be so engrossed in playing their instruments that they will not notice when you change the cards. Encourage the children to watch all the time while they are playing. It will also help to give them turns as conductors, so that they can see the importance of responding to the cards.

Notation

Assessment opportunities

This activity enables you to assess children's ability to respond to visual symbols, to identify and control instruments, and to take control as conductors.

Opportunities for IT

Some programmes include instrument pictures which can be used for this activity, and it may be possible to assign a suitable sound to each picture when it is displayed on the screen, so that the sound is heard each time the child clicks on the picture.

Display ideas

The children can draw their own instrument pictures for display, and can put these into sequences as simple compositions for others to try.

Reference to photocopiable sheets

Photocopiable page 138 shows the instruments used for this activity. (You can draw additional pictures if you wish.) The Conducting sheet (page 114) may also be useful when teaching signals for starting and stopping.

Moving forward

This activity leads directly into 'Signs and cymbals' (page 98), in which the instrument pictures are replaced by simple symbols used in the same way. You can also extend this activity by experimenting with different sounds on each instrument, and choosing a specific sound for each group to play in response to the appropriate card. The use of instrument pictures can also be extended to 'Grid notation' (page 106), when the pictures can be used to represent sequences of instrument sounds with a steady pulse.

SIGNS AND CYMBALS

To develop awareness of the use of abstract symbols to represent instrument sounds.

†† *Whole class.*

🕐 *15 minutes.*

♪ *Medium.*

Previous skills/knowledge needed

The children need to be very familiar with instrument cards before moving on to the use of symbols explored here. The activity follows on directly from 'Instrument pictures' (page 96).

Key background information

One of the things which puts teachers (and children) off using notation is the mystery of what the symbols represent. Any form of notation, whether formal or informal, can seem like an impenetrable code, understandable only to the favoured few. This activity uses simple symbols, based on the shapes of the instruments themselves, as a way of introducing a code system which can be easily understood and followed. The activity follows exactly the same sequence as 'Instrument pictures' (page 96).

Vocabulary

Drum, triangle, tambourine, cymbal, instrument.

Preparation

Prepare a set of cards from photocopiable page 138 in exactly the same way as you did for 'Instrument pictures'. If you want to use a wider range of instruments than those provided on page 138, you will have to devise your own symbols for them. Have a collection of drums, triangles, tambourines and cymbals (and other instruments if you wish) ready for the class to play.

Resources needed

The set of instrument cards from photocopiable page 138, the set of symbol cards from photocopiable page 139 and one instrument per child.

What to do

Sit the children in a circle and remind them of the work they have done with the instrument cards in the previous activity. Hold the instrument cards up, one at a time, and ask the children to identify the instruments shown. Explain that you are going to show them a new set of cards, which still tell you to play the same instruments, but instead of pictures they have a symbol for each instrument.

Show them the new cards one by one, then spread both the instrument cards and the symbol cards out on the floor in the centre of the circle, and ask the children which symbol card they think matches each instrument card. The symbols are devised to echo the shape of the instruments:

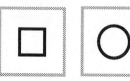

| drum | tambourine | triangle | cymbal |

Notation

Now take the instrument cards away and ask the children if they can remember which symbol represents which instrument.

Give out the instruments, allow a minute or two for the children to play freely, then stop them and use the symbol cards to conduct each group exactly as you did with the instrument cards in 'Instrument pictures' (page 96). Conclude the lesson by asking some of the children to take turns as conductors.

Suggestion(s) for extension

Children who have grasped the idea of using symbols to represent sounds can devise their own symbols and use them to create simple compositions, or they could use the symbols given here in the same way.

Suggestion(s) for support

Some children will find it hard to grasp the abstract nature of these symbols. It may help them if you hold both the instrument card and the symbol card up for each group so that they can see the link between the two.

Assessment opportunities

This activity enables you to assess the children's understanding of the use of abstract symbols to represent sounds, their ability to control instruments in response to these symbols and to act as conductors.

Opportunities for IT

The computer should be a useful tool for generating high-quality symbols to use in this activity. Children could extend this work by using multimedia authoring software to link the sound and the symbol together. The sounds could be taken from collections of sounds stored on the computer, from CD-ROMs, from a keyboard linked to a computer via a midi interface or by recording sounds with a microphone plugged into the computer.

The software could be arranged so that each screen contains the symbol for an instrument and then possibly an ear picture (icon) so that when the children click on the ear they hear the sound of the instrument. Older children could add to a simple collection set up in advance by the teacher.

Display ideas

Copies of the symbol cards can be displayed alongside the corresponding instrument pictures. Sequences of the symbols can also be displayed with an invitation to the children to try playing them.

Reference to photocopiable sheets

Photocopiable page 139 shows the four symbols used for this activity. (You can devise additional signs of your own if you wish.) The cards made from photocopiable page 138 are also used in this activity.

Moving forward

This activity links well with 'Graphic notation' (page 100) and 'Grid notation' (page 106), both of which use abstract symbols to represent sounds. Symbols of this sort are also used to represent rhythmic patterns in 'Percussion band' (page 52). Children might also use symbols of this type to record compositions they have already made or to generate new ones.

GRAPHIC NOTATION

To introduce and use the concept of graphic notation

†† *Whole class, then small groups of four or five.*

🕐 *30 minutes.*

♫ *Medium.*

Previous skills/knowledge needed

'Starting and stopping' (page 14) offers the children experience of responding to symbols when playing instruments. 'Instrument pictures' (page 96) reinforces the use of shapes to indicate instruments, while 'Signs and cymbals' (page 98) uses symbols to represent instruments.

Key background information

The understanding that a sign or symbol indicates that a particular sound should be made is basic to the concept of notation. A range of symbols can be used; perhaps the formal notation system of Western classical music or even freely-drawn patterns devised by the children. Numbers, note names or instrument shapes might also be used.

Graphic notation is used to express and write down sounds that have already been chosen and ordered. It is the most actively artistic form of notation as the shape, size, even sometimes the colour will have an effect on how the notation represents the sound.

Vocabulary

Symbol, sign, graphic, notation, pattern.

Preparation

Find a screen or board behind which you can play an instrument without being seen. The door of a cupboard or an upturned table would be fine. Assemble a box of different-sounding instruments and cover it with a cloth or coat. Collect a further selection of tuned and untuned percussion instruments – one for each child. Collect a number of thick felt-tipped pens or crayons, and prepare a display space where the children will be able to see the graphic notation as they are working from it. Make one copy of the Graphic score sheet (page 140) for each child.

Resources needed

One Graphic score sheet (page 140) per child. A4 paper for trying out graphic symbols, a large sheet of A3 paper for drawing whole-class graphic notation, tuned and untuned percussion instruments, a box with a cover, screen, crayons or felt-tipped pens, means to stick up graphic notation sheets.

What to do

Seat the children so that they can see you and, before giving each one an instrument, remind them that they mustn't let their instruments speak until you say it is time to play. It is worth being firm about this as it means that this and future lessons will run very smoothly with more time for music and fewer interruptions. As soon as all the children have got instruments, ask them what the starting and stopping signs are ('Starting and stopping', page 14). If the children have had experience of this, ask a child to conduct the class in starting and stopping. Giving the children time to play their instruments at the beginning of the session means that they will be ready to listen as you move on to the work with individual sounds.

When the class has had some playing time, go behind the screen and play a single sound on one instrument, a bang on a drum or a tinkle on a triangle. Ask the children what sort of sound they heard. Ask them specific questions such as:

▲ Is it a loud sound or a soft sound?

▲ A smooth sound or a spiky sound?

▲ A short sharp sound or a long booming sound?

Give out the paper and ask the children to tell you how they would make a pattern to show the sound that you have just played. Ask individual children to draw some ideas for patterns for the sound.

The concept of drawing an abstract sign can be difficult, so emphasise that it is a pattern you want rather than a picture of everyone playing, because that would take too long to draw. Draw a few examples of squiggles to give the class some ideas.

Choose one of the patterns and tell the children that this is the sound that you just played. Now play another instrument behind the screen and repeat the process. Do this four or five times but increase the number of instruments being played by asking a few of the children to play at the same time. When you feel that the class is confident with this give out the A4 paper and ask *everyone* to play at the same time. Ask them how they could show this on their paper.

Give them time to draw the symbols, then show a few examples to the class and practise pointing and playing. Discuss whether they like the sound of everyone playing together.

Now tell the children that they are going to make up a class composition using this method. Ask how they want to start, with a single instrument, a group, or the whole class. Using the examples that the children have already tried, draw in the appropriate symbols on the A3 sheet, as directed by

the children, and then prepare for the first performance with you, or a child, pointing at the large score.

Once the children have experienced this form of notation they can compose their own music in groups of four or five and record it on the Graphic score sheet (page 140). You could set up this activity so that it continues throughout the week, with small groups working in the instrument corner, or you could continue the whole-class activity by rearranging the order of the existing symbols and introducing a few new instruments, then playing another performance.

Suggestion(s) for extension
Children who find the activity easy could be asked to use more than four symbols within one composition and extend the length of the notation from which they play.

Suggestion(s) for support
Children who find the activity difficult could be asked to conduct when all the children are playing. They will then experience what happens when they point at a symbol and what happens when they take their finger off the same symbol. This will give them greater confidence when performing themselves.

Notation

Assessment opportunities

This activity provides opportunities to assess how well children understand the concept of notation and their ability to represent something in an abstract form.

Opportunities for IT

The children could use an art or drawing package to create their notation system. They could then go on to create their own scores using the same software, giving these to other children to play.

Younger children could use a concept keyboard linked to a drawing package so that when they select a symbol on the concept keyboard overlay it appears on the screen. A similar approach could be taken using framework software like *My World 2* with an appropriate set of symbols created by the teacher in advance.

One alternative would be to use a multimedia authoring package to link the notation to the actual sounds so that clicking on the various notation symbols would result in the score being played.

To do this children would first need to design the symbols and save them on to a disk so that they could be used later. They would then need to use a microphone linked to the computer to record a sound for each of the symbols. Next, they would need to import the symbols and arrange them to make their composition, finally linking the symbols to the soundbites so that when a user clicks on a particular symbol she hears the sound for that symbol. The children need to know how to import their notation symbols, and make the links to the appropriate sound file.

Reference to photocopiable sheet

Photocopiable page 140 provides space to record a composition graphically.

Display ideas

Graphic notation always makes a colourful and eye-catching display. Use photographs or the instruments themselves to link the notation to the actual instruments represented. Display the composition as a whole and, if you have taped the finished product, have that available to listen to so that the whole project makes sense to the audience. Invite them to make up their own notations and compositions.

Moving forward

Repeat the activity as many times as you wish, every time the children use graphic notation their ideas will become more complex and subtle. 'Making waves' (page 74) uses graphic notation to represent a composition once it has been composed. 'Mini orchestra' (page 55) invites children to write down their compositions in their own way.

MUSIC CORNER CARDS

To introduce children to a range of ways of representing pitch, volume and duration.

†† *Whole class or groups of four to six, then individuals, pairs or small groups.*

🕐 *15–20 minutes to introduce each of three sets of cards.*

🎵 *Medium.*

Previous skills/knowledge needed

The children need to be aware of high and low, loud and quiet and long and short sounds. The relevant activities from the Basic skills chapter would provide a good preparation for this. Before using the pitch cards, it would be useful to have tried 'Pitch dance' (page 34) and 'Raindrops' (page 94). 'Sounds in a circle' (page 28), 'Adventures in sound' (page 44) and 'Composition cards' (page 69) would all provide useful background experience for the volume and duration cards.

Key background information

This activity presents three sets of cards which demonstrate some of the ways in which informal notation can be used to represent *pitch* (high and low sounds), *volume* (loud and quiet sounds) and *duration* (long and short sounds). The symbols on the cards are fairly self-explanatory – a long mark for a long sound, a wavy line for a sound which alternates between high and low, and so on – but the exact way in which you interpret the symbols is up to you and the children. There are no right answers in this activity, and no right ways of using the cards.

Each card is marked either pitch, volume or duration, but when you have run through this activity a few times, you might like to try swapping them around to see whether the symbols work for other elements (whether a pitch card, for example, works for volume).

Vocabulary

Pitch, high, low, volume, loud, quiet, duration, long, short

Preparation

Select the set of cards you want to use from photocopiable pages 141 to 143 and make four photocopies of the ones you have chosen. (It is advisable to introduce one set at a time, to avoid confusion.) Cut up your chosen sheets, stick the pieces on to cards and cover them with clear adhesive film. Get out a range of instruments if you plan to use them (see 'Resources needed').

Resources needed

Four sets of your chosen cards (see 'Preparation'). All the cards can be used with voices and bodies alone, but you may like to provide some tuned instruments for pitch and a selection of tuned and untuned instruments for volume and duration. If you *do* use instruments, provide enough for the whole group or class.

What to do

Introduce your chosen cards either to the whole class or to one group at a time. Tell them what the cards represent (pitch, volume or duration) and ask them for suggestions as to how they might 'read' them. Ask for some volunteers to demonstrate their ideas using voices, bodies or instruments if you have provided them, and discuss their interpretations with the rest of the group or class.

So, for example, the volume card might be interpreted as a series of claps getting louder or quieter, while the pitch card could be a voice sound that starts high and slides down.

Now ask some volunteers to hold up four cards at the same time, for the rest of the class or group to read. These can either be four identical cards (the same card from each set), in which case the result will be a discernible repeating pattern, or a combination of different cards from the same set, which will give a less predictable, but very interesting, effect.

Nominate some of the children as conductors, to lead the rest of the group or class through the patterns you make in this way. When you have explored a range of combinations, you can give the cards to a group (or several pairs) of children

Notation

to explore on their own. The cards can then be kept in the classroom music corner for children to use independently, working either individually, in pairs or in small groups.

Suggestion(s) for extension

Children who have grasped the concept of using these notation cards can devise their own cards for others to use. They can also experiment with instruments to see which are the most suitable for each set of cards.

Suggestion(s) for support

Some children will find it hard to grasp the relationship between the marks on the cards and the sounds they might represent. It will help these children if you draw large-scale versions of each card on the board and ask them to come and 'conduct' from these enlarged symbols while the rest of the class make the corresponding sounds. This will enable them to 'feel' the sounds at the same time as hearing them.

Assessment opportunities

This activity provides opportunities for you to monitor children's ability to relate sounds to symbols, to follow a conductor and to act as conductors themselves.

Opportunities for IT

The children could use a drawing or an art package to create their own symbols for this activity. They could also use a multimedia authoring package to assign a sound to each of the symbols. (See suggestions in 'Graphic notation' on page 100).

Display ideas

Copies of the cards can be displayed with an explanation of their use or, if the children have made their own versions, these can be displayed with an invitation to come to try them.

Reference to photocopiable sheets

Photocopiable pages 141 to 143 provide three sets of notation cards: one for pitch, one for volume and one for duration.

Moving forward

The children can make use of the patterns on the cards to record compositions they have already made (perhaps in activities in the *Composing* chapter) or to generate new compositions. If they have not yet tried 'Graphic notation' (page 100) this would be a good time to do it, as it explores similar ideas to those used in this activity. Even if they *have* already worked through 'Graphic notation', they could revisit it with the benefit of increased knowledge.

Notation

READING A SONG

To develop children's awareness of formal notation.

†† *Whole class.*

🕐 *15–20 minutes.*

♫ *Medium.*

Previous skills/knowledge needed

It would be helpful if the children had experimented with some aspects of informal notation before starting this activity. 'Raindrops' (page 94) is particularly relevant, as it introduces the principle of pitch notation.

Key background information

You do not need to be able to read music to carry out this activity. The intention is to demonstrate the very simple principle that every sound in music is represented by a mark on the page, and that by following the marks one by one you can follow the melody of a tune or song. Using this principle, you will find that it is possible for young children to 'read' a familiar song without knowing what notes the marks represent, just as it is possible for them to 'read' a familiar story without recognising the words on the page.

Vocabulary

Long note, short note, running notes, minim, crotchet, quaver, stave.

Preparation

Draw five evenly-spaced lines on the chalkboard (the width of a metre ruler is about right) and copy the tune of 'I hear thunder' (or 'Frère Jacques') from photocopiable page 144 on to the five lines (known as a staff or stave). Take care to copy the notes exactly as they appear on the sheet: some are between the lines, while others have a line running through them. Some are filled in, others are empty; some are joined to others, some stand alone. If you have a photocopier with an enlarging facility, you may prefer to enlarge the sheet to A3, instead of drawing the tune on to the board.

Resources needed

Photocopiable pages 144 and 145, a long pointer (perhaps a metre ruler or a large piece of paper rolled into a taper).

What to do

Sit all the children where they can see the chalkboard and, without telling them what the song is, start singing it while pointing to the notes you have drawn on your stave (photocopiable page 145 shows how the words relate to the notes in case you are unsure). After the first few words of the song, pause, and ask the children what the next word is (they should know the answer because they know the song), then invite them to continue singing as you point to the notes. Sing through the song two or three times in this way, pointing to the notes at all times.

Now invite individual children to come and be conductors: tell the rest of the class that they must follow the conductor exactly, and that if the conductor slows down or stops, they must do the same. Make this into a game by suggesting that the conductors try to catch the class out by stopping, speeding up or slowing down at unexpected times. Children get an enormous sense of power through controlling the class in this way, so a turn as conductor is very popular.

After you have sung the song in several different ways, with different conductors, look at the notes on the stave with the children and ask whether they notice any differences between them. They may point out differences in shape or shading. Sing the song through again and stop at the first 'you'. Point out that this note looks different because it is a long note (called a minim) in the song. Sing it again to demonstrate the short notes (crotchets) of 'I hear thunder' and the long note of each 'you'. Move on to 'Pitter patter raindrops' and point out that these short notes (quavers) go even faster than the ones at the beginning of the song: they are often called running notes, and are joined together by tails or cross-bars. Finally, ask the children either to sing or to clap through the song again while you point to the notes.

Suggestion(s) for extension

Children who take to this activity very easily can go to look for their own favourite songs in song books and sing them to you or to friends, pointing to the notes as they sing.

Suggestion(s) for support

Some children may lack confidence in following the line of the music, and seem uncertain about what is going on. Often the best remedy for this is to make the least confident child into the conductor, thus giving her the opportunity to discover how she can stop and start the music by staying still or moving on to the next note.

These children will also benefit from looking for and singing through their favourite songs in song books, as this will reinforce the one-to-one correspondence between the notes which are sung and the written notes.

Assessment opportunities

This activity provides ample opportunity to assess children's understanding of the principles of formal notation, as well as their skills and confidence in singing and conducting.

Opportunities for IT

Any IT music program which plays back musical notes when they are entered on an on-screen stave is ideal for reinforcing the skills and concepts introduced here. Children can hear the notes individually as they enter them, then see and hear how each note on the stave is represented by a sound when they play back the whole sequence. The sequence can then be printed out and displayed.

All Acorn RISCOS computers come with *Maestro*, a free piece of software, which could be used for this activity.

Display ideas

Favourite songs can be displayed on the wall or in a class book and then sung in the children's free time. A large wall display of a song or tune with an accompanying pointer will give numerous opportunities for children to practise pointing to the notes, both individually and in groups.

Reference to photocopiable sheets

Photocopiable page 144 gives the tune only of 'I hear thunder' while photocopiable page 145 provides the tune with the words. Both can be used for the children to read independently or for display, as well as for the initial stimulus for this activity.

Moving forward

Once you and the children have grasped the basic principle of formal notation through this activity, you can select your own favourite songs to read in the same way. You can use the melody line from any familiar song for this, but if you are copying from a song book with piano accompaniments, make sure you only copy the top line of notes, as this will be the tune of the song. The children can also adapt some of the ideas learned here for use in notating their own compositions.

GRID NOTATION

To introduce and develop the principle of grid notation.

♯♯ *Whole class and small groups of four or five.*

🕑 *Two 30-minute sessions.*

♫ *Session One: medium.*
   Session Two: advanced.

Previous skills/knowledge needed

The children would benefit from experience in playing sounds from symbols. 'Instrument pictures' (page 96) outlines a way of making a symbol from an instrument sound. 'Cut-and-paste composing' (page 60) uses this idea as a basis for composing.

Key background information

In music notation there is an assumption that a steady pulse underlies the music and that the notation is read in the context of that steady pulse. The music might be going faster or slower than the pulse, but the notation directs this and indicates whether it is a strict halving or quartering of the pulse that is required or whether the music merely runs slower or faster than the pulse.

Notation

It is important that children grasp the idea that a steady beat lies behind the notation. This activity introduces this through the use of a 4-square grid, and develops it through the use of a 16-square grid in Session Two.

The symbols that are used for notation can vary greatly. Formal notation is only one method and pictures of instruments that the children wish the player to use or symbols representing the instruments may be more appropriate. Cubes of different colours could be used to represent different sounds or particular note names, or the note names themselves could be used. There is no right or wrong approach. What is important is that the children understand that different symbols represent different and very specific sounds. In this activity the graphic notation symbols are used, but any other set of symbols could, and should, be used as the activity is repeated again and again.

Vocabulary

Pulse, grid, symbol.

Preparation

Choose what sort of symbols you are going to be using for the session. As mentioned above these could be simple instant signs, such as a cross drawn to represent a clap and a foot for a stamp, or highly artistic graphic representations of a sound. Produce, or have ready the means to produce, these symbols.

For Session One you will require copies of the 4-square grid (page 146), enough for one per group of four or five children, plus four or five copies to experiment with as a whole class.

Similar numbers of copies of the 16-square grid (page 147) are required for Session Two.

Resources needed

Photocopy enough grids to use in the lesson. If you wish to reuse the sheets, cover them first with clear adhesive film before drawing the symbols on them with felt-tipped pens. You will then be able to rub out the symbols and reuse the grids many times.

If appropriate, make an enlarged version of each grid so that everyone will be able to see them clearly in a whole-class session.

What to do
Session One

Seat the children so that they can all see the 4-square grid. Explain that they are going to play music by reading what is on the grid. Reassure them that you will show them how to read the grid. Next, explain the need for them all to start together so that every member of the class is playing the same part of the music at the same time. Tell them that you are going to point to each square in the grid and as you point to each square you want them to say 'point'.

Start the class reading the grid at the same time by holding your finger away from the grid as you count '1, 2, 3, 4' slowly and steadily. As soon as you have said '4' point your finger to the four squares in turn (keeping the same pulse as the '1, 2, 3, 4'), saying 'point' each time your finger touches the square. Repeat this a few times so the children become used to the idea.

If the children seem happy with this tell them you would like to make it more interesting. Ask them whether they want to use claps or stamps. According to the answer draw either four squiggles (stamps) or four stars (claps) on to the grid. Ask them what they think the squiggles (or stars) mean.

Emphasise that they are now going to stamp (or clap) because that is what the symbol tells them to do. Count them in as before '1, 2, 3, 4', then point to each square in turn in time to the pulse. If this is successful repeat it, using a child from the class to point to each square instead of you, although you may have to support the child in keeping the rhythm of the pulse.

If the children are still confident with this, tell them that you are going to make it more exciting still. Take a new grid and draw on it three squiggles (or whatever sign you used last time) and one vertical straight line. Ask the children what they think this sign means, then explain that the vertical line is a slap on the thigh. Count the children in to play the new layout as before, but make sure it is kept at a steady, fairly sedate, pace. Again point to each of the squares, keeping to the same time as the pulse. Check that they act according to the symbols and include the single slap on the thigh at the right place. Having done this, again ask a child to conduct the class.

If the children remain confident ask one of them to write the symbols on a new grid, this time arranging the symbols in a different order. Challenge the class to play this new composition, and take note of whether they seem to be generally confident in playing according to the symbols or whether they just play randomly.

As a final performance, play through all the grids that you have made.

Session Two

Remind the children of the work that they did in the previous session and, using one of the children as conductor, play through some of the compositions from the previous session.

Explain that you are now going to make the activity a little more complicated.

Show the class the large grid of 16 squares. Ask the children whether they have any ideas on how they think they could use it for composing. If you get interesting suggestions other than those in the activity then try them out, if at all possible.

Otherwise, take up the idea of extending the practice of drawing symbols into the squares and then playing the piece according to the symbols, just as before. To fill 16 squares you may want to think up a wider range of symbols and sounds, or you may wish to use instrument sounds with new symbols thought up by you and the class. As in the previous session, rehearse the playing by pointing to each square in turn in time to a steady pulse.

When you start playing from the filled-in grid you may find that the children have trouble coping with blank squares or rests. Rehearse these parts separately by playing to just before the blank square and continuing a couple of squares beyond it. Blank squares at the ends of lines are particularly difficult and should be avoided initially.

When the class is confident with the new-size grid, split them into groups of four or five and ask them to make up their own group compositions. You can give specific instructions about what can and can't be used (perhaps slaps, clicks and claps, or only instruments that you shake) or you can let them choose their own sounds.

Suggestion(s) for extension

If children find this easy, introduce the idea of having two claps or sounds to a square. This would be shown by drawing two symbols in each square and played by clapping twice quickly in the same time as one of the 'normal' pulse claps.

Suggestion(s) for support

If children are finding the concept hard to understand, repeat the activity in Session One with them using one symbol only and pointing to each square as they play it.

Assessment opportunities

This activity enables you to assess whether a child is able to follow and understand the concept of notation and to keep a steady beat.

Opportunities for IT

The children could use a drawing package to create their own musical scores. They could also use a multi-media authoring package in which the graphical notation is linked to a library of sounds so that they compose and play simple scores using the software. Some commercial software such as Topologika's *Music Box* or *Compose World* can be used in similar ways to experiment with these ideas of graphical notation.

Display ideas

Display the grids that you have used in a place where the children can read them. Invite them to play these and make up further notations of their own to play.

Reference to photocopiable sheets

The 4-square grid sheet is on page 146 and the 16-square grid on page 147.

Moving forward

Repeat the activity with the children working independently in pairs or small groups. 'Graphic notation' (page 100) develops the use of abstract symbols to represent sounds. Once the children have mastered playing from a grid they can use this in 'Show time' (page 72) or in other activities in the *Composing* chapter. This activity links well with 'Mini orchestra' (page 55) and 'Talking about music' (page 88) in which the children are asked to analyse what they have played and listened to.

Assessment

This chapter sets out what we see as the fundamental principles of assessment in music: that it happens all the time, that every activity is an assessment activity, and that assessment is primarily about noticing what children are doing.

These ideas are explored in a little more depth, and a range of practical recording formats are offered, which you can use or adapt as you wish.

Specialists will continue to argue about whether, and how, music should be assessed for years to come – that argument cannot be resolved here, but the chapter offers some down-to-earth suggestions on how to make the most of what you notice – and gather some useful evidence for OFSTED inspections into the bargain.

ASSESSMENT IN MUSIC

Many teachers worry even more about assessing music than about teaching it. Musical skills and understanding are so nebulous that it often seems impossible to define them or pin them down. To make matters worse, children may show extraordinary levels of skill on one occasion, and then appear to have lost them altogether on the next. (Witness the proud teacher who asks her class to play their composition in assembly, only to find that it has turned into an uncoordinated disaster!)

If you have anxieties about assessment in music you should remember the following points.

▲ Assessment in music happens all the time. You do not need to do extra assessment activities to find out what your pupils have learned.

Every activity in this book can be used as an assessment activity, and every time you notice something a child is doing in music, you are carrying out assessment. The points most likely to emerge are listed in the Assessment opportunities at the end of each activity, but you should also be on the lookout for the unexpected. You may notice something that will only happen once. Children with special needs will often shine unexpectedly in music when they find it hard to achieve in other areas.

▲ Assessment doesn't have to be written down

Assessment should *not* be confused with recording. Most of the 'assessment' you carry out will simply consist of noticing and responding to what the children are doing. It may, however, be useful to keep a record of the most significant points, as this will be of great help when you need to report to parents, other teachers and the children themselves on their progress. Four different ways of recording this information are offered here. These are designed to suit different teacher's styles and preferences (see 'Recording sheets' on page 111).

▲ There is no National Curriculum requirement for formal assessment in music.

There are no primary music SATs, and teachers' own assessment is not reviewed by external moderators. However, you *are* required to make yearly reports to parents, and to undertake a summary assessment at the end of each Key Stage, based on the end of Key Stage Statements in the National Curriculum document.

This is made much easier (especially for the harassed Year 2 teacher!) if a brief musical profile is built up gradually throughout the Key Stage: if a series of 'snapshots' has been compiled over the years, you should have a very useful general picture of the child's musical development by the end of Year 2. Records of this sort will also provide the kind of evidence OFSTED want to see – of musical progression taking place through a range of experiences, supported by a

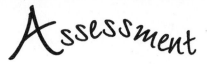

Assessment grid — has shown that he/she

Through classroom activities

- can act as leader in a musical activity
- is confident in conducting
- can start and stop playing in response to a conductor
- can respond to different signals from a conductor
- can explore voice sounds
- can control the pitch of own voice
- can control the tempo of own singing and movements
- can control own voice to create long and short sounds
- can recite words rhythmically
- can distinguish between verse and chorus in a song
- is aware of different singing styles
- can sing along with a recorded song
- can sing in tune with someone else
- is confident in singing
- can control instruments
- can control the volume of instruments
- can hold and control a beater
- can control the quality of sound produced
- is aware of everyday objects as instruments
- is aware of how sounds are produced
- can repeat a melodic pattern (tune)
- can memorise a melodic pattern (tune)
- can distinguish between different melodies
- can keep a steady beat
- can move in time to music
- can keep a beat independently of others
- can copy a rhythm
- can memorise a rhythmic pattern
- can create a rhythmic pattern
- can perform simple rhythmic patterns

Reporting prompt sheet

Name

Composing
- composes using instruments
- composes using voice and body sounds
- uses rhythm to compose
- uses melody to compose
- makes use of skills learned
- can use simple notation to record own compositions
- is able to revise and extend compositions

Playing/performing
- sings with enthusiasm
- concentrates when playing
- can follow or act as a conductor
- shows or is developing skill in playing instruments
- can keep time with a group
- can keep a simple rhythm going
- shows awareness of other players when performing
- starts a performance with silence
- ends performance 'professionally'
- has an awareness of audience
- can follow simple notation (formal/informal)

Listening and appraising
- enjoys listening to different types of music
- can talk about own and others' work
- can listen sensitively and with concentration
- has opinions about different sorts of music
- uses a wide vocabulary to talk about music
- is aware of rhythm/melody/dynamics /tempo/timbre/texture
- is developing awareness of structure in music

- is a
- can create m
- (using more than one
- can plan a performance
- can play as a member of a group
- can listen to other players while performing
- is confident in performing
- is aware of music's potential to create an atmosphere
- is aware of others' music-making
- is sensitive to others' music-making
- can evaluate own performance
- can evaluate others' performances
- can apply skills learned (in composing/performing)
- can listen carefully to music
- can talk about music
- can use abstract symbols to represent sounds
- can follow graphic notation
- can understand grid notation
- can follow grid notation
- is aware of the principles of pitch notation
- is aware of the principles of formal notation

useful and usable assessment and recording system. Other suitable forms of evidence are recordings of the children's work, photographs, videos, pictures, and anything the children say or write about their work in music.

Recording sheets

We offer four different types of recording sheets here. These are intended to bridge the gap between the Programmes of Study and the End of Key Stage Statements, but you may prefer simply to use the wording of the National Curriculum document itself.

The first set of recording sheets (photocopiable pages 148 and 149) simply summarise all the points raised in 'Assessment opportunities' throughout the book. These have been grouped to show how they relate to each other, but you will find that every activity in the book addresses a whole range of items on the list. These sheets can be used as a checklist to provide an at-a-glance record for the whole class. This could be updated perhaps termly or half-yearly, to reflect the developing skills of your pupils.

Alternatively, you may prefer to use the reporting prompt sheet (photocopiable page 150) which follows. This is a summary of the kinds of comments you might make about your pupils' progress, grouped under the National Curriculum headings.

The third option is a more open-ended assessment and reporting sheet (photocopiable page 151) which offers space to make observations on individual children's progress in ten key areas of music. You can use one sheet for each child, to build up an individual musical profile throughout Key Stage 1 years.

Finally, photocopiable pages 152 to 157 provide a range of self-assessment sheets which the children can use on their own, or with a little help from you. The first three sheets (pages 152 to 154) can be used to evaluate a single activity in composing, performing or listening, while the second set of three (pages 155–157) are summary sheets which children might use towards the end of a term or year. All these sheets can be kept as evidence of the children's musical progression, along with samples of their completed photocopiable sheets from some of the other activities.

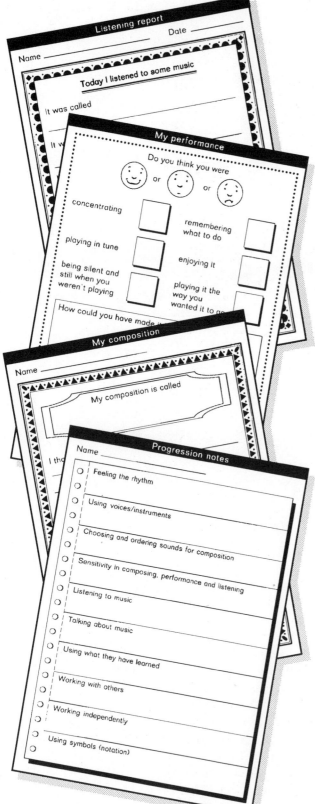

Photocopiables

The pages in this section can be photocopied for use in the classroom or school which has purchased this book, and do not need to be declared in any return in respect of any photocopying licence.

They comprise a varied selection of both pupil and teacher resources, including pupil worksheets, resource material and record sheets to be completed by the teacher or children. Most of the photocopiable pages are related to individual activities in the book; the name of the activity is indicated at the top of the sheet, together with a page reference indicating where the lesson plan for that activity can be found.

Individual pages are discussed in detail within each lesson plan, accompanied by ideas for adaptation where appropriate – of course, each sheet can be adapted to suit your own needs and those of your class. Sheets can also be coloured, laminated, mounted on to card, enlarged and so on where appropriate.

Most pupil worksheets and record sheets have spaces provided for children's names and for noting the date on which each sheet was used. This means that, if so required, they can be included easily within any pupil assessment portfolio.

Photocopiable sheets 148 to 157 may be used for the purposes of summative assessment and are discussed in the Assessment chapter.

Starting and stopping, see page 14 (see also pages 15, 16, 18, 19, 20, 22, 23, 24, 25, 96)

Conducting sheet

Start...

or

or

choose your own favourite way.

STOP

or

like a policeman...

LOUD!

quiet

↑High

↓Low

Multibeat, see page 38

Multibeat animals

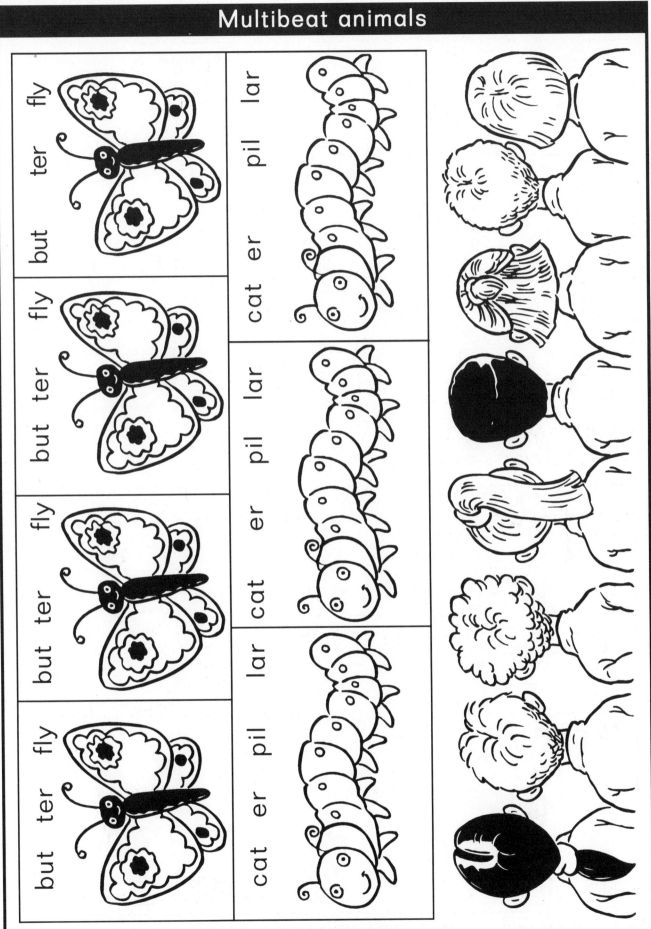

Multibeat, see page 38

Multibeat sounds

fly ter but	lar pil cat er	u ig
fly ter but	lar pil er cat	don o an u ig
fly ter but	cat er pil lar	
fly ter but	lar pil er cat	don o an u ig

Greasy chips, see page 41

Greasy chips

grea

sy

grease
grease
grease
grease
grease
grease
Greasy

greasy

gr gr gr gr ee e aa s s s yyy

greeeeaas

greasy

y

gr **ea** sy

ea

greasy

gr

sy

gre**asy**

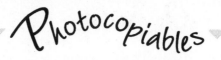

Percussion band, see page 52

Percussion band cards: 1

Percussion band, see page 52

Percussion band cards: 2

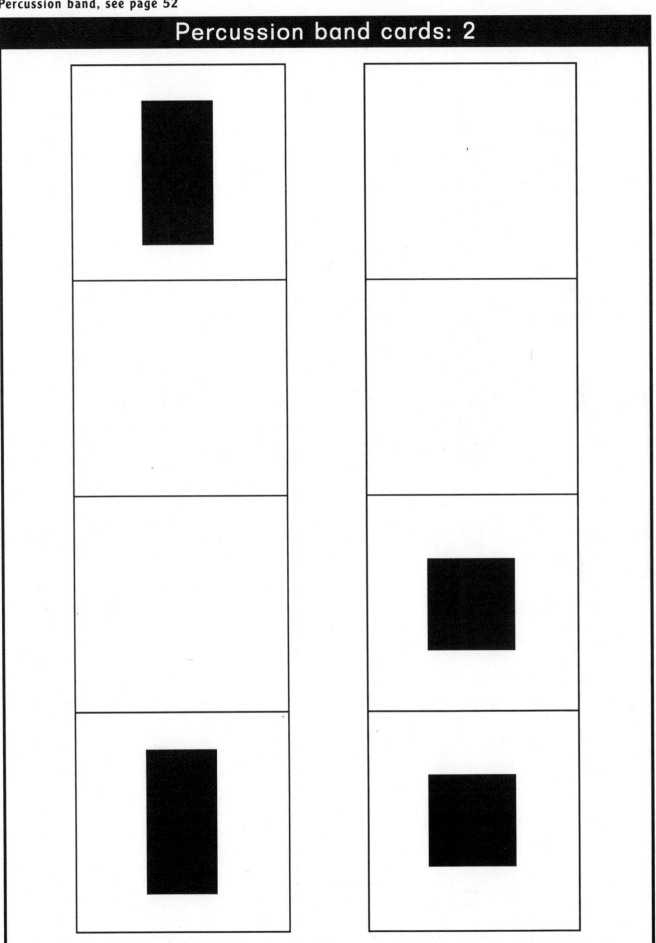

MUSIC

Percussion band, see page 52

Percussion band grid

Instruments of the orchestra

Cut-and-paste composing, see page 60

Instruments: 1

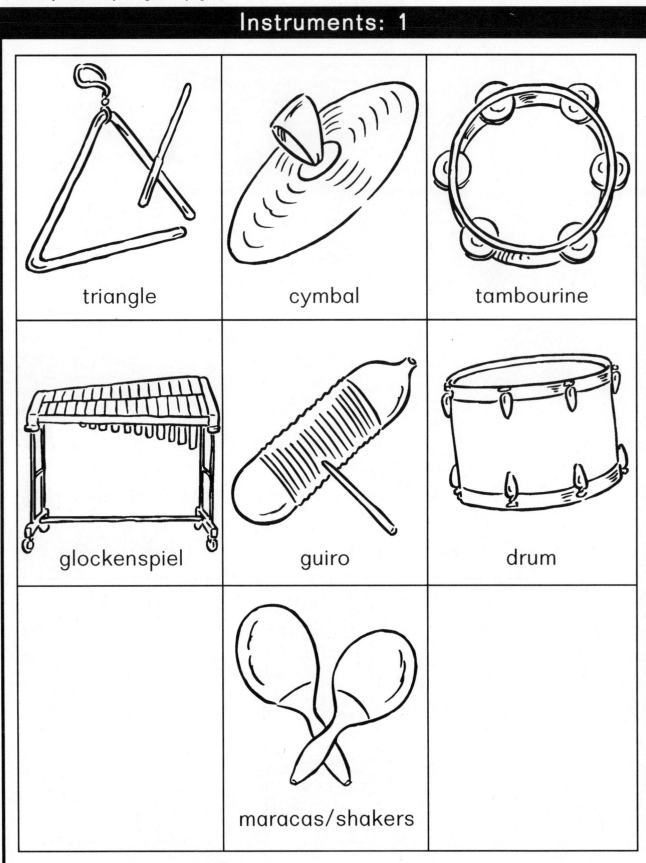

triangle

cymbal

tambourine

glockenspiel

guiro

drum

maracas/shakers

▲Choose the instruments you want.
▲Cut them out and stick them on to the composition sheet.

Cut-and-paste composing, see page 60

Instruments: 2

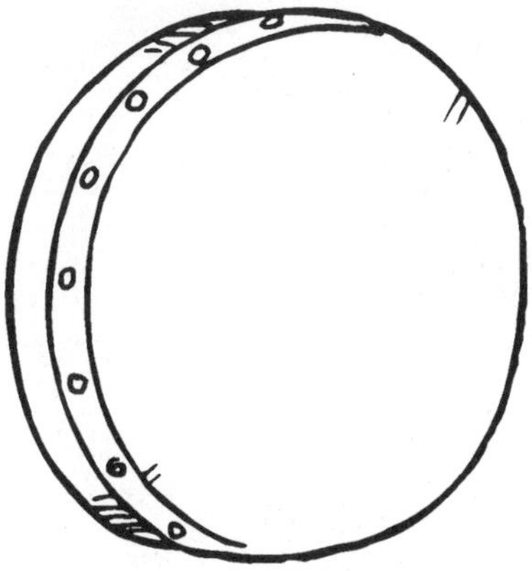

tambour

bongo drums

cowbell

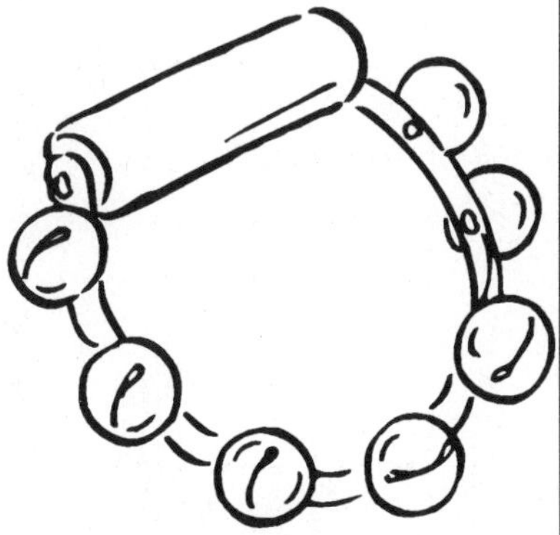

bells

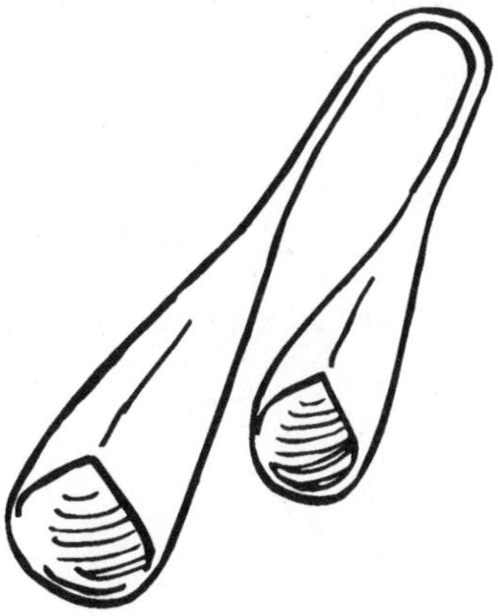

ago-go

xylophone

temple bells

▲ Choose up to four instruments.
▲ Cut them out and stick them on to the composition sheet.

Cut-and-paste composing, see page 60

My composition

MUSIC

Building a sound house, see page 64

Sound house

Building a sound house, see page 64

My sound house

Name _____

Composition cards (level 1)

individual
pair
group

Level 1

Make up a composition
which gets
louder and then quieter.

---

individual
pair

Make up a
composition
using two
instruments.

Level 1

---

individual
pair
group

Level 1

Make up a composition using
high sounds and low sounds.

---

individual
pair
group

Level 1

Make up a composition
using your voice.

Composition cards, see page 69

Composition cards (level 2)

†† individual pair

Level 2

Make up a tune using five different notes.

†† individual pair group

Level 2

Make up a composition using \\\\|///sounds‗— and silence. SSSSsshh!

†† individual pair group

Level 2

Make up a composition using l o n g and short sounds.

†† pair group

Level 2

Make up a composition using different types of sound.

Composition cards (level 3)

individual
pair
group

Make up a composition with a rhythm and a melody.

Level 3

---

individual
pair
group

Level 3

Make up a composition with a

beginning, a middle and an end.

---

group

Make up a composition using several different instruments at once.

Level 3

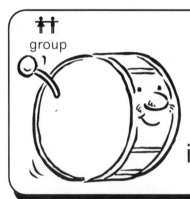

---

group

Level 3

Make up a composition for several voices.

Show time, see page 72

Game board

Show time, see page 72

Board game record sheet

Name _____   Date _____

Game 1

Game 2

Game 3

Show time, see page 72

Board game instructions

 = chime bars   = drum   = choose any instrument

 = tambourine   = hand sound

| Instrument swap | = swap an instrument with someone

| practise | = you may practise for one minute.

Game 1

When you land on an instrument square 'collect' that instrument, by drawing it or writing its name on the recording sheet. When you get back to the start practise your composition. The **winner** is the first person to reach the stage and perform his or her composition.

Game 2

Collect instruments as you move around the squares on the board. Compose a rhythm for your instruments. Record this in the box on the recording sheet. The first person to reach the stage and perform a composition with rhythm on the instruments is the **winner**.

Game 3 – (play in pairs)

Move around the squares on the board, collecting instruments as you go. Compose two different rhythms that would sound nice together and practise playing these. The first pair to reach the stage and perform their composition are the **winners**.

MUSIC

Jazz band line-up

Talking about music, see page 88 (see also page 35)

Music words

smooth

quiet

jolly

booming

rrrrepeating ggggg

tuneful

boring

spiky

LOUD

happy

bold

harsh

jumpy

slide

calm

Talking about music, see page 88

Listening opinion sheet

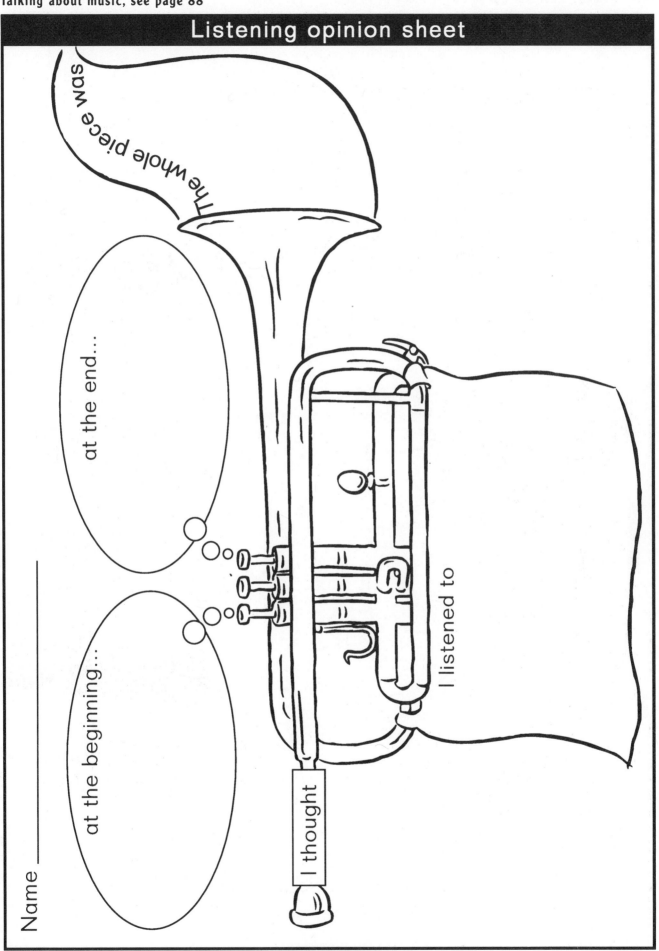

The whole piece was

at the end…

at the beginning…

I listened to

I thought

Name

Making waves, see page 74

Listening comparison sheet

We listened to two compositions...

One was called

The other was called

The composition was about...

This is how it started...

...it ended...

This is what I thought of it...

Marks ____
10

Marks ____
10

Raindrops, see page 94

Raindrops notation

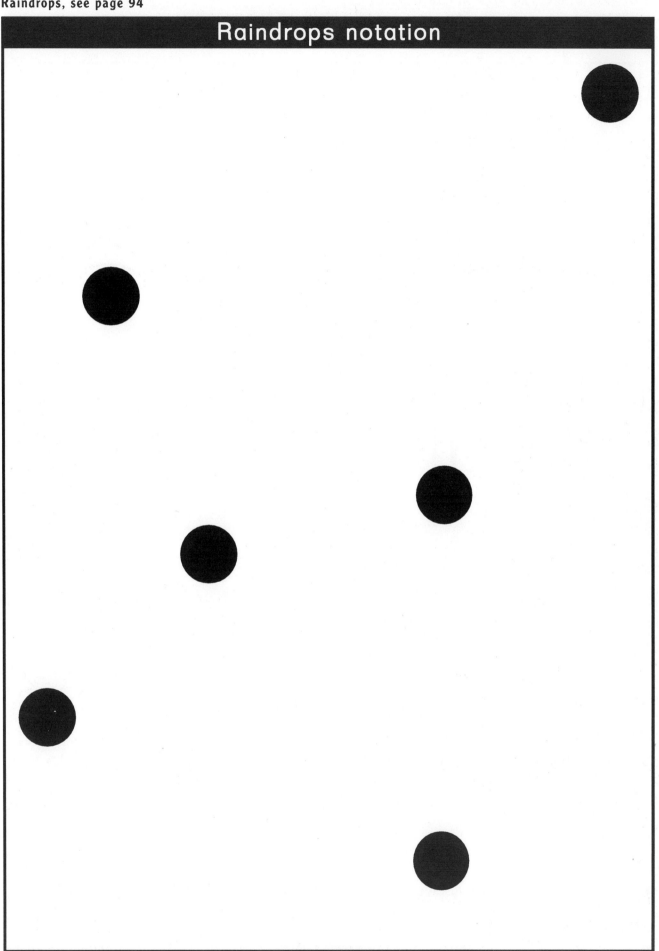

MUSIC

Instrument pictures, see page 96 (see also page 98)

Instrument pictures

Signs and cymbals, see page 98

Instrument symbols

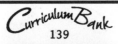

Graphic notation, see page 100 (see also page 35)

My graphic score

Name _____

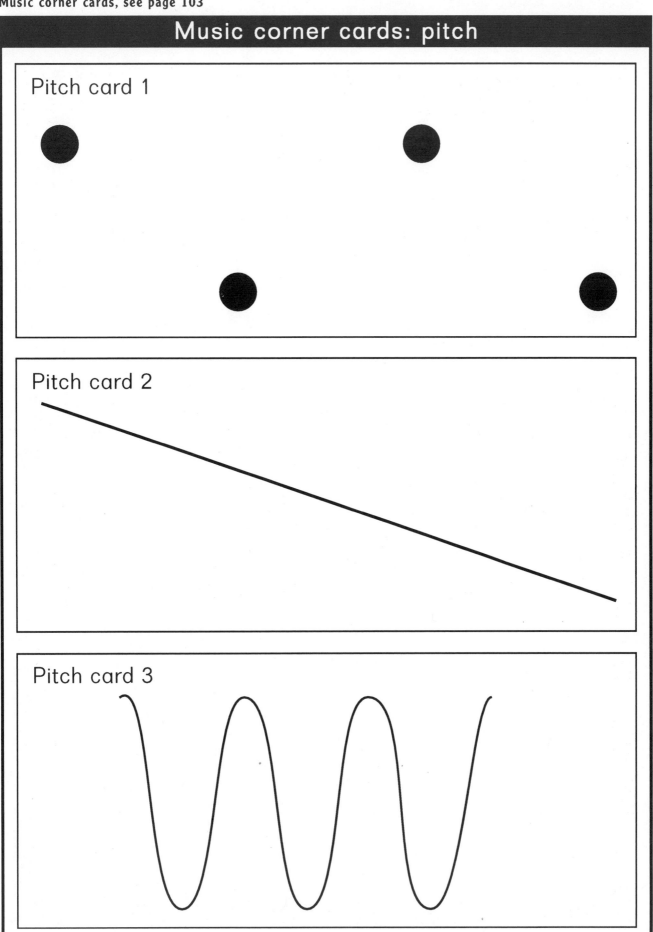

Music corner cards, see page 103

Music corner cards: volume

Volume card 1

Volume card 2

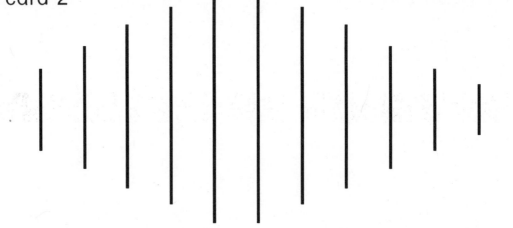

Volume card 3

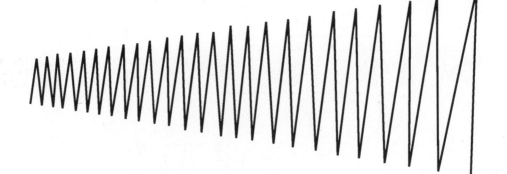

Music corner cards, see page 103

Music corner cards: duration

Duration card 1

Duration card 2

Duration card 3

Reading a song, see page 105

Photocopiables

Reading a song

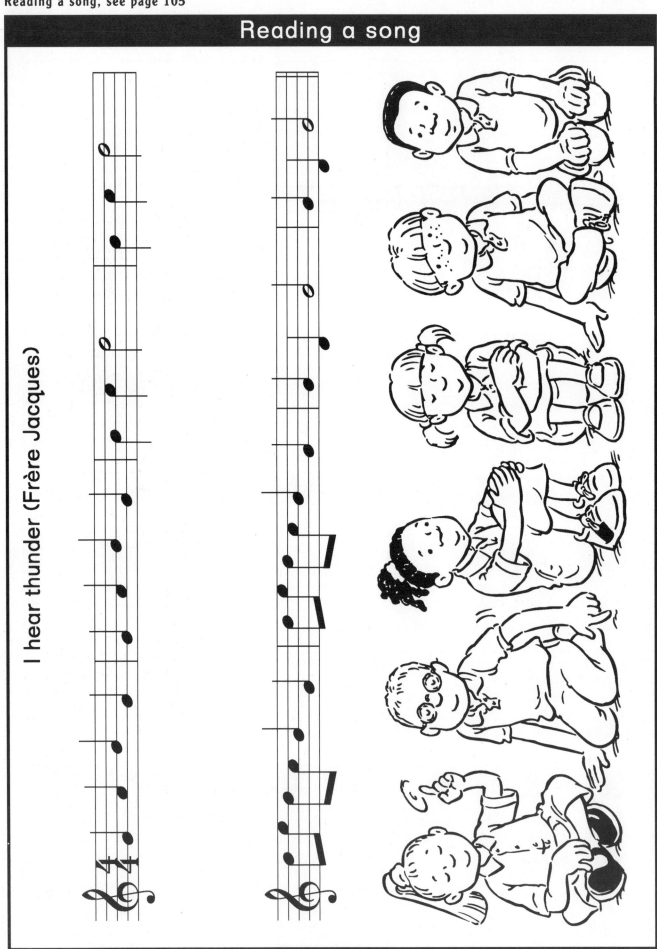

I hear thunder (Frère Jacques)

Reading a song, see page 105

Reading a song

I hear thunder (Frère Jacques)

I hear thun - der, I hear thun - der, Hark don't you? Hark don't you?

Pit - ter pat - ter rain drops, Pit - ter pat - ter rain drops, I'm wet through, so are you.

Grid notation, see page 106

4-square grid

Grid notation, see page 106 (see also page 52)

16 square-grid

Assessment grid, see page 111

Assessment grid

Through classroom activities _____ has shown that he/she

can act as leader in a musical activity					
is confident in conducting					
can start and stop playing in response to a conductor					
can respond to different signals from a conductor					
can explore voice sounds					
can control the pitch of own voice					
can control the tempo of own singing and movements					
can control own voice to create long and short sounds					
can recite words rhythmically					
can distinguish between verse and chorus in a song					
is aware of different singing styles					
can sing along with a recorded song					
can sing in tune with someone else					
is confident in singing					
can control instruments					
can control the volume of instruments					
can hold and control a beater					
can control the quality of sound produced					
is aware of everyday objects as instruments					
is aware of how sounds are produced					
can repeat a melodic pattern (tune)					
can memorise a melodic pattern (tune)					
can distinguish between different melodies					
can keep a steady beat					
can move in time to music					
can keep a beat independently of others					
can copy a rhythm					
can memorise a rhythmic pattern					
can create a rhythmic pattern					
can perform simple rhythmic patterns					

Photocopiables

Assessment grid, see page 111

can play a rhythm independently of others					
is aware of multiple rhythms					
is aware of timbre (different sounds)					
can describe timbre					
is aware of texture (combination of sounds)					
can describe texture					
can use rhythmic patterns in composition					
can use melodic patterns in composition					
can use voices in composition					
can use words in composition					
is aware that composing involves ordering sounds					
is aware of structure in music (beginning, middle, end)					
can create more complex compositions (using more than one of the elements above)					
can plan a performance					
can play as a member of a group					
can listen to other players while performing					
is confident in performing					
is aware of music's potential to create an atmosphere					
is sensitive to others' music-making					
can evaluate own performance					
can evaluate others' performances					
can apply skills learned (in composing/performing)					
can listen carefully to music					
can talk about music					
can use abstract symbols to represent sounds					
can follow graphic notation					
can understand grid notation					
can follow grid notation					
is aware of the principles of pitch notation					
is aware of the principles of formal notation					

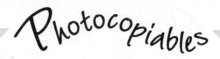

Reporting prompt sheet, see page 111

Reporting prompt sheet

Name

Composing

composes using instruments

composes using voice and body sounds

uses rhythm to compose

uses melody to compose

makes use of skills learned

can use simple notation to record own compositions

is able to revise and extend compositions

Playing/performing

sings with enthusiasm

concentrates when playing

can follow or act as a conductor

shows or is developing skill in playing instruments

can keep time with a group

can keep a simple rhythm going

shows awareness of other players when performing

starts a performance with silence

ends performance 'professionally'

has an awareness of audience

can follow simple notation (formal/informal)

Listening and appraising

enjoys listening to different types of music

can talk about own and others' work

can listen sensitively and with concentration

has opinions about different sorts of music

uses a wide vocabulary to talk about music

is aware of rhythm/melody/dynamics /tempo/timbre/texture

is developing awareness of structure in music

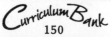

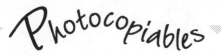
Progression notes

Name _____

○ | Feeling the rhythm

○ |

○ | Using voices/instruments

○ |

○ | Choosing and ordering sounds for composition

○ |

○ | Sensitivity in composing, performance and listening

○ |

○ | Listening to music

○ |

○ | Talking about music

○ |

○ | Using what they have learned

○ |

○ | Working with others

○ |

○ | Working independently

○ |

○ | Using symbols (notation)

○ |

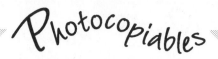

My composition

Name _____

My composition is called

I thought the best part was

_____

_____

_____

I thought the worst part was

_____

_____

_____

My friends thought the best part was

_____

_____

_____

signed ....

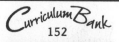

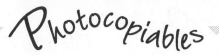

My performance, see page 112 (see also pages 32, 55)

My performance

Do you think you were

😊   or   😐   or   🙁

concentrating ☐

remembering what to do ☐

playing in tune ☐

enjoying it ☐

being silent and still when you weren't playing ☐

playing it the way you wanted it to go ☐

How could you have made it better?

My performance, see page 112 (see also pages 32, 55)

MUSIC

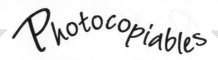

Listening report

Name _____   Date _____

Today I listened to some music

It was called

_____

It was composed by

_____

It was performed by

_____

Here are three words to describe what it sounded like

_____

_____

_____

I thought it was

brilliant ☐   ok ☐   didn't like it ☐

signed ....

These are a few of my favourite things!, see page 112

These are a few of my favourite things!

My favourite
song is

My favourite piece
of music is

My favourite classroom
composition is

signed ....

MUSIC

My music assessment sheet, see page 112

My music assessment sheet

Name _____

Things I am good at

_____

_____

_____

This is me doing it

Things I find hard

_____

_____

_____

This is me trying to do it

My favourite thing in music is

_____

_____

_____

My picture of it

This is the music I have enjoyed listening to, see page 112

This is the music I have enjoyed listening to

Date I heard it	What it was called	Where it comes from

INFORMATION TECHNOLOGY WITHIN MUSIC

Music is predominantly a practical subject and children need to experiment with sounds, instruments and voices. However there are opportunities for teachers to use different forms of information technology to extend children's experiences in a number of ways which will develop their musical skills as well as contribute to the development of their IT capability.

Music software

There are already a number of specific packages for music which help children explore sounds, rhythms, composition and notation. Ensure that these are appropriate to your pupils before bringing them into the classroom as they may not develop music as it is taught in the school. Some of this software enables children to explore different sounds made by the computer. These can be based on instrumentals or the children can create their own 'voices' by changing the parameters of the sound. Some software uses pre-set sounds while others allow children to select sound phrases and join them together to make their own music.

Packages like *Compose World* have a range of sound phrases in different styles. These are represented graphically and children can create their own music by selecting and linking them together on a grid, making their own compositions and exploring musical patterns. Other software such as *Music Explorer* allow children to select individual notes represented in graphic notation on the screen. Many packages also have a rhythm section where children can set up different rhythms using a range of instruments.

There are numerous notation packages available. These range from the simple to the very complex. You should be aware that many of these are full notation systems unsuitable for younger children.

Art and drawing packages

A number of simple art or drawing packages, suitable for children, are available across a wide range of computers. These can be used when children are exploring or designing their own music notation systems. The software tends to fall into two categories.

The first are drawing packages which enable children to draw lines and shapes and add text. The lines and shapes can be manipulated, by resizing, moving, stretching and rotating them. Colours can be changed and shapes filled.

On more sophisticated packages individual shapes can be combined to form a single object so, for example, all the symbols in a phrase of music can be drawn separately and combined as a single phrase which can be copied and moved around the screen. These packages make it easy to move shapes around the screen and position components of the music wherever you wish. Text can also be added.

Art or painting packages use a different approach, but can often achieve the same or similar results. The drawing process is closer to using a pencil or brush. Very detailed work and special effects can be produced to create pictures which mirror the results of paint on paper. These packages usually have a range of tools such as brushes, sprays and rollers for adding and creating different effects. Text and shapes can be added, coloured and resized.

The skills that children need to be taught to use such software are similar to those needed for word processing, but related to pictures. They will need to know how to:
▲ select appropriate drawing tools;
▲ change features such as line thickness;
▲ draw different lines and shapes;
▲ edit and erase shapes and lines;
▲ resize and rotate shapes and lines;
▲ move shapes and lines around the screen;
▲ select and add colours;
▲ add, resize and colour text;
▲ save and retrieve work from a disk;
▲ set up the printer and print out the work.

Multimedia authoring software

This software allows different pages or screens of information to be linked together. Depending on the way that the links are created children can move to different parts of the presentation by clicking with a mouse on a symbol, word or picture. Such presentations usually begin with a title page and this allows the user to move directly to different sections.

Another important feature is the software's ability to handle a range of different information including text, pictures from art and drawing packages, digitised pictures from scanned images and pictures from clip art. It can also handle sounds samples which can be recorded using a microphone linked to the computer and special software. Sounds can also be taken from audio CDs or commercial sound collections and, where schools have keyboards and a midi interface, sounds may be taken from the keyboard and saved as a sound file on the computer.

These recorded sounds can be used in many activities where children are creating simple compositions or linking musical notation to sounds so that by clicking on the symbols they have used the actual sounds are played.

The data files created by this type of work can be very large, so a computer with a hard disk and adequate memory is needed. If the final presentation is to be moved to other computers via a floppy disc this will also limit the number of pages, pictures and sound clips that can be included.

Work with authoring packages is best undertaken as part of a longer project. A class presentation can be divided between several groups with each one preparing the text and pictures for their own section and deciding how the pages are to be laid out and linked. Children could also work as a single group to record and notate their own composition.

The grids on this page relate the activities in this Curriculum Bank to specific areas of IT and to relevant software resources. Activities are referenced by page number; bold page numbers indicate activities which have expanded IT content (in relation to a specific area of IT). The software listed is a selection of programs generally available to primary schools, and is not intended as a recommended list. The software featured should be available from most good educational software retailers.

AREA OF IT	SOFTWARE	ACTIVITIES (page no.s)					
		CH 1	CH 2	CH 3	CH 4	CH 5	CH 6
Communicating information	Word processor		38, 41	44		84, 86	94
Communicating information	Art package		35, 38		74		94, 98, 100
Communicating information	Drawing package		35, 38	49, 55	60, 62, 67		94, 98, 100, 103
Communicating information	CD-ROM					81	
Communicating information	Authoring software			46	60, **64**, 74		96, **98**
Control	Tape recorder		30				
Communicating information/Control	Keyboard		32		64, 67		

SOFTWARE TYPE	BBC/MASTER	RISCOS	NIMBUS/196	WINDOWS	MACINTOSH
Word processor	Pendown Folio	Pendown Desk Top Folio	All Write Write On	Word for Windows Kid Works 2 Creative Writer	Kid Works 2 EasyWorks Creative Writer
Art package	Image	1st Paint Kid Pix Splash	Paint Spa	Colour Magic Kid Pix 2 Fine Artist	Kid Pix 2 Flying Colours Fine Artist
Drawing package		Draw Vector Art Works		Claris Works Oak Draw	Claris Works
Multimedia authoring		Magpie Hyperstudio Genesis		Genesis Hyperstudio Illuminus	Hyperstudio
Music	Compose	Compose World Music Box Music Maker	Compose	Music Box Music Explorer Music Maker	Thinkin things – Toony Loons

Cross-curricular links

	ENGLISH	MATHS	SCIENCE	HISTORY	GEOGRAPHY	ART	D&T	PE	RE
BASIC SKILLS	These are basic skills in music which transfer to other subject areas but are not cross-curricular by nature.								
USING VOICES AND BODIES	Using nursery rhymes. Using story.	Dividing rhyme into 4 (1/4). Counting in 4s. Counting in 3s. 4s, 5s.	Healthy/unhealthy food.	Dance and dance music from the past. Songs and nursery rhymes that granny sang.	Indian vocal rhythms. Indian classical music. African drumming.	Collage of different representations of voices playing and singing.	Making a metronome for keeping a steady beat.	Body movements for high and low.	Sacred song and dance across the world.
USING INSTRUMENTS	Poems describing sounds that instruments make. Writing about instruments.	Rhythmic and melodic patterns. Counting in 4s.	Types of sound that different articles make.	Researching different instruments used in different periods of history.	Instruments used in different parts of the world, similarities and differences.	Observational drawing of instruments. Collage of people playing instruments e.g. Jazz Band collage.	Using everyday instruments for different purposes.	Responding to different instrument sounds in movement. Creating shapes of different instruments in dance/PE.	Appreciating extraordinary talents in people, e.g. Evelyn Glennie (deaf percussionist).
COMPOSING	Using theme tunes from cartoons (media studies). Following written instructions.	Making patterns and sequences. Using a dice.	Composition about science topics.	Compositions about different history topics e.g. The coming of the Romans.		Drawing what is in our house. Art inspiring music, painting a picture of the sea.	Cutting and sticking.	Using class compositions as a stimulus for movement.	Representing different sacred stories in sound.
LISTENING	Descriptive vocabulary expressing opinions.	Listening for sets of beats.	Listening to hear how sounds are made, different types of sound.	Early jazz, America 1920s. Music from different times 1728 Beggars Opera.	Listening to West African drumming. Listening to Indian vocal music.	Painting in response to listening.	Survey of all the machines that we use for listening. Assessing sound quality.	Moving in time to music. Running round in circles.	Music as part of Hindu festival. Link between ragas and Hindu mythology.
NOTATION	Notation and its relation to codes. Code-cracking games.	Use of symbols to represent music.				Abstract representation of sound.			